FROM LINDOS AND BEYOND

{Diamond Destinations}

The third 'From Lindos' novel

'From Lindos and Beyond'

Copyright Josephine Kelly.2022

First published by Lulu.com 2022

The right of Josephine Kelly to be identified as the author

of this book is registered. All rights are reserved. Please do not copy without prior permission of the author.

A British Library catalogue record for this book is available

ISBN NO. 978-1-716-04753-4
Imprint: Lulu.com

Typeset Calibri 10.

Formatting Jamie O'Donoghue, Zakir Afridi.

Front cover Paul Nicholls, back cover Viv Dare.

FOREWORD

At the time our story starts it was still possible to travel the world as one chose. People flew abroad for business on a regular basis and took holidays to distant lands.

Before Brexit, and the pandemic, news in the English papers and on the television was mild by comparison. But one issue managed to gain European attention.

The Hatton Garden Diamond Heist.

You may ask

How did an event in London affect our friends on Rhodes? Read on.

PROLOGUE   APRIL 2015

JOHN NIGHTINGALE CLOSES the courtyard door and walks briskly down the narrow, cobbled streets, negotiating the uneven flights of steps with ease. He is on his way to Giorgos bar in the centre of the medieval village of Lindos. There he will join the group of 'expat' workers enjoying an all-day breakfast.,

'Kalimera, tikaneis', he asks no one in particular.

He knows most of the early morning customers and is aware that they will be too busy drinking their first coffee of the day to stop and answer the polite enquiry.

'Kalimera Johnny, kala, eisai?' It is Eleni who replies. He takes his usual seat and dumps his rucksack onto the chair next to him. His Greek coffee and 'all day' breakfast already being prepared.

John has been back on Rhodes Island for three weeks, and a small stone house in the medieval village of Lindos is where he calls home and a place to call home is important to John. As a child he travelled the world with his father's R.A.F. postings, but in many ways, he still leads the nomadic life. John had just returned from Austria, where he spent the past five months teaching skiing. Then in the summer he runs a water sports business in Kiotari.

After the traditional morning greeting, Tsambikos, Eleni's husband, turns the television on. Even though it is still too early for most of the tourists, the bar is busy with workers of every and any nationality. And now, at breakfast time, they like to scan the BBC news, even if only for the football results. Tsambikos selected the channel.

The news reader announced.

'We go to our home affairs correspondent, who is in Hatton Garden this morning'.

'Turn it up a bit please?' John asks. 'Wow, did you see this?'

Usually a very quietly spoken man, the fact that his voice was raised was enough to draw everyone's attention. Tsambikos adjusted the volume, wondering what the fuss was about.

'During the weekend, a robbery has taken place in Hatton Garden, the diamond dealing area of London. Thieves broke into the steel vaults and have escaped with more than a million pounds' worth of jewels and gold, taken from safe deposit boxes. Scotland Yard is investigating how the theft, which must have taken at least two days and nights to execute, went unnoticed'.

'Not me mate, been here all week', John laughed. 'What would anyone do with that sort of money? And how would you change it into cash to start with. No thanks, I'm alright as I am. Can I have another coffee please Eleni?'

Tsambikos' lovely wife took the empty cup and put it into the basket for washing. A clean one was placed under the coffee machine. John had been living in Greece long enough to enjoy the thick, dark beverage. No Nescafe for him.

'You are right, about the diamonds, I think the same', Eleni told him whilst waiting for the cup to fill. 'If you have your health, you have everything'. She was quite content with what she had.

Eleni had inherited the popular Giorgos café, known to all as Georgios, from her father. It occupied a prime position in the village, and the natural right angles at the junction of three lanes formed a courtyard style seating area. Over the years Tsambikos and Eleni had modernized the interior, providing plush bar stool seating and dining tables for those who wished to eat. The menu was simple and inexpensive; good Greek food with the addition of the 'all day' English breakfast.

Eleni and her husband ran the place between them, with help from her sister, Ioanna, and Tsambikos' brothers, Stephanos and Leo and Jacob, who helped in the busy summer months. Jacob and his wife also had a second bar on Pallas beach, named appropriately Giorgos Two.

John Nightingale stood near the till to pay his bill, and once that was done, returned to the table to pick up his rucksack.

'Right, I'm off', John announced. 'See you tonight, same time, same place'. There were various calls of 'see yer', and 'later', from those still in the bar.

Many years ago, John had started a successful water sports outlet on Pallas beach. But for the past few years he had managed a water sports venue in Kiotari, owned by a large German hotel.

'It is great, no tax or insurance to arrange, all I do is turn up, do the job I enjoy, and collect my money at the end of the month', he told anyone who wanted to know. But he kept his little house in Lindos, as he enjoyed the social scene there.

As he left the bar he bumped into Tanya.

'Kalimera, tikaneis'? She laughed at the Greek greeting and responded with a fake north of England accent. 'Great mate, how yers doin'. John gave her a hug. 'Everything ready for the craft group. Plenty of glitter and glue?' he teased her.

'Well as ready as I will ever be. Not going to panic. It is the first time on my own, but I watched my aunt June teaching for the past couple of years, so it will be fine'. He wished her the 'best of British', and as he went to his car for the drive down the island, Tanya joined the customers in the bar. She sat at the far end, and after ordering her usual Nescafe and croissant, opened the laptop. There were a couple of emails that needed answering. The main thing was that there were no cancelations from the holiday guests. And just as important, no last-minute requests to join the course.

She did not bother to look at the news.

****

THEODOSIS MARKOULIS ALREADY HAD GUESTS booked into The Mystic, his bijou hotel in the centre of Rhodes Old Town. The type of clients he attracted were more interested in the architecture than spending all day on the beach, and early April, was an ideal time of the year for that type of holiday.

He had daily newspapers in the small bar, changing his choice depending on the nationality of his guests, though these days, most people read English, regardless of their background.

He glanced at the headlines of all three papers, The Daily Mail, La Repubblica, Der Freitag. They carried the same news.

'A multi-million-pound diamond robbery in London'.

For many people the world over, there was something exciting about such an audacious bank robbery. It was not in the same class as robbing an old man and stealing his few euros.

The Italian couple from Turin came down into his reception lounge.

'Buongiorno, oggi non vogliamo colazione, grazie. Prendiamo il traghetto per l'isola di Symi'.

'You are going to Symi? Siete sicuri? Nemmeno un caffe?'

'No grazie, buona giornata'.

'Buona giornata, have a good day'.

I would have made breakfast earlier if only they had asked, he thought. *But what can you do if they do not say?*

Theo shrugged his shoulders, betraying his years studying in Rome. He always wanted his guests to have the best experience possible when staying at his hotel. He returned to the newspapers; fascinated by the way the news of the robbery was reported in the different countries.

****

ON SYMI ISLAND, JAMES COLLINS rarely bought a paper, he read what he needed to online. Even then he only bothered with the Guardian, never the tabloids. He wrote a blog, Symi Dreams, and mixed catching up with the news, and his novel writing, into his daily stint on the laptop. He, and his photographer partner Neil Gosling, had been on Symi for almost eighteen years. Neil had a photographic shop, selling his cards and calendars of Symi, its scenery and its cats. And James' books.

The books, some novels, some travel guides, promoted their beautiful Greek home, attracting an ever-growing group of tourists each year.

'Wow, that took some doing', James remarked, more to himself than to Neil, though Neil was there in the kitchen where the Mac was open on the table.

'What now, another story of someone selling a million books, featuring a lady detective, set in the jungle outside Luton?'

'No, a diamond heist, in the middle of Hatton Garden', James replied, ignoring the smart remarks.

'Wow! how come they could get away with that with CCTV and security and everything, that is amazing!' he added. 'I will read it later. I am going to the shop. Can you think of anything we need for this evening? Remember we are going out to another meeting for Solidarity Symi tonight. We might as well eat after that'.

'Yes, certainly, not a problem'.

Sometimes James wondered when the people of Symi would be able to close the charity group set up to help the thousands of refugees arriving on the Greek islands over the past three years. But there were still places that had boats landing almost every day, and Solidarity Symi were now forwarding some of their surplus clothes, tents, and waterproofs to help other islands around the Dodecanese.

James read through the rest of the article, thinking what a crazy world it was, when some people had diamonds in boxes and others put their children in boxes to keep them safe.

******

IN THE SOUTH OF ENGLAND, SIMON grabbed a jacket and walked out the door of their Folkestone guest house. He enjoyed getting the paper every morning. It gave him a reason to walk along the sea front, take in the fresh air, be it a rainy or sunny start to the day. He had lived by the coast most of his life, as a child in his native Devon, and for the past thirty years in his adopted Kent. The shifting colours of the sea and sky never ceased to amaze him.

They usually only bought the Daily Mail, but this morning Geoff asked him to buy most of the papers available. This Simon did for the next few weeks, and as the names came into the frame Geoff told him what he knew about the men in question. Who they were, how long he had known them, what form they had, and his surprise, or otherwise, at them being involved in anything that organised as the diamond heist, or not organised, as more details emerged over the next few days.

Truth be known, Geoff had more than a casual interest in the men in the frame, as one of them owed him some money. Not a lot, but it seemed unlikely he would be picking up that debt for some time now, if ever.

Some you win, some you lose. I hope my contact details are not in his place. Nothing to do but sit and wait, he thought.

They usually went out on a Friday night. Nothing fancy, just along to the Fisherman's Rest, where they had a fish and chip supper and a couple of pints. Simon always let Geoff call the shots, and depending on how the older man felt, they came home at about half past nine, or stayed on till eleven. Geoff did not feel safe walking out on his own. His knee was causing a problem. They had picked up a wheelchair at a house sale a few weeks ago, but only for days when he did not feel so good.

It might seem rather a rum existence for Simon, a man in his early fifties, but Sy had no complaints. After all the years of running their small guest house it really was a piece of cake. He saw his daughters on his birthday, and on theirs, and again at Christmas. He was content, more than content, and regardless of what had happened years ago, he always considered he owed old Geoff. He would not let him down now, not when he needed someone to push the wheelchair.

Simon never was involved with the London business, and he hoped that his friend's interest in the diamond heist was only for old time's sake. Nothing more, nothing less.

****

IN BARCELONA, DAVID sat at the desk in his mother's house. He was checking his emails. David had applied for summer work with the Waterhoppers diving school on Rhodes, and yes, here was the email to confirm he had the job.

He helped himself to cereal, careful to wash his dish after he had eaten. His mother had enough to do, teaching all day. He did not expect her to be clearing up after him.

David took his coffee into the small study and opened his laptop. He was in the last year of his degree in architecture. His next plan was a Ph.D. in maritime archaeology. Now with the summer job in Rhodes, he would aim for a PADI teaching certificate. Then he could travel anywhere in the world and follow his love of maritime history.

He rang his friend Hratasha. Yes, she was also returning to Rhodes in the summer. Hritasha was from Kolkata, India, but studying psychology in Athens. There was news of Kyle, her South African boyfriend, and others from last years' gang.

The Spanish papers were still reporting on the diamond robbery in London.

'Who needs diamonds'? he said to the cat, as she took up her usual seat on the sofa beside him.

****

HEATHER HAD FINISHED HER PACKING. She had pared down her belongings when she went back to Scotland to live with her parents, Shirley and Ken. They had recently moved to a small modern bungalow in Dalkeith, just outside the city of Edinburgh, where she had grown up.

So, Heather had not a lot of choice about what to take with her to Greece. Her main concern was leaving everything neat and tidy for her mother. Shirley was looking after her two-year-old grandchild, Lucy, for the week, and Heather wanted to make everything as easy as possible. She checked her list again. Nappies were the priority. Maybe Lucy should be dry by now, but the upheaval of moving, leaving her husband and home in Manchester, left Heather with little energy to be thinking of things like that. Her Dad had laughed, 'Don't worry, it will all be the same by the time she is twenty-one'. Ken hoped this week away would do Heather some good. No point if she was worrying about Lucy.

And all though she did not know it at the time, for Heather, the week in Greece would become quite an adventure, leading to her and Lucy living on Rhodes. A year later, she would be waiting for her dad to visit them in the village of Asklipios. Diamonds! What diamonds?

****

IT WAS MANY YEARS SINCE NIGEL LAWRENCE had been to Greece. Many years since, as a penniless drifter, he had sold doughnuts from a tray, walking the beach each day to earn enough for a meal and a bed. It was the age of the hippies, of squatting, and working where you could for a few quid.

And along that journey, when searching for his father's family in Canada, he met a group of

Pentecostal Christians, and his life changed forever. Now, some forty years later, he planned to take a break from his home near Calgary, though not from his ministry.

It was more than a year later, on his way back through Europe, couch surfing with friends on the way, he arrived on Rhodes. The diamonds he carried in his luggage were copies of the New Testament, and a few sheets of his favourite hymns, ready to photocopy when he reached his destination. Prasonissi.

****

IN STOWE, BUCKINGHAMSHIRE, RUTH Wallis had slept in later than usual. Though it was almost a week since she had finished the last days of her teaching career, she was still quite exhausted. There had been so much to do those last few weeks. Cupboards to clear ready for the new member of staff who would take over her class after Easter. Hats for the end of term play, and spare pants, just in case there was an accident. No one else would wish to inherit her treasure trove.

But that was all behind her now. She could indulge in a lazy morning if she so chose. And today was one of those mornings. But she had things to do. Soon she would be off to Greece for a craft holiday. And she had yet to decide what to take with her, and having decided, she would need to pack.

Ruth had not seen or read about any diamond heist, and if she had it would have been of no interest at all. She possessed just an ordinary, plain phone. It did what phones were supposed to do. It made and received phone calls. Yes, she had a television, and watched the six o'clock news. She would have seen about the robbery, but it caused her no further thought. London and its criminal fraternity were as foreign to her as the Greek island of Rhodes where she would spend a ten-day break.

The events in London were to change the lives of those involved.

In a totally different way, Ruth would change her life beyond her wildest imagination.

******

LORD BERTRUM RAWLINS walked the land of Chilham Grange with his nephew, Marcus. They stopped in the early morning sunshine and leaned on a gate. The Kent countryside was stunning. Certainly, there were times when Bertie, as he preferred to be called, wondered why he spent so little time in his own back yard. But, although there were occasions when his signature was needed on a legal document, technically it was no longer his back yard. He had signed the whole estate over to his nephew some years ago.

Now there was a French wine company offering to buy part of the land, as it adjoined their main purchase in the area. Bertie had told Marcus the decision was his. This visit to talk about the issue was, in Bertie's eyes, a curtesy discussion. Nevertheless, he was pleased that Marcus had asked his advice. They got into the four by four and returned to the house where lunch was ready.

Bertie had already packed, as later that afternoon he would drive up to Heathrow and catch the flight back to Rhodes. Strange, but he felt more at home there than in Kent. He had picked up the Guardian from the hall stand, as something to read on the flight. The diamond heist caught his eye in the headlines, but nothing could be further from his mind. Thankfully, not his problem.

****

And as we know …. 'What a difference a day makes,

    only twenty-four hours.

        How things may change in a year!

PART ONE.

ALTHOUGH IT WAS MORE than a week since teaching her first Lindos craft group, Ruth was still quite exhausted.

It was the late nights and eating out more than the teaching, she reasoned to herself. She stretched lazily, relishing the comfortable bed and the luxury of not having any commitments today. But used to a lifetime of discipline, she felt quite guilty indulging in the extra hour in bed.

The bedroom was so beautiful, with the light streaming in from the window and the bougainvillea peeping through the shutters.

Ruth had showered last night, when the water had been warm from the solar panel, so just a sloosh sufficed, and naturally, clean her teeth.

The courtyard was bright and sunny. She took her coffee and toast outside and sat in the warm morning air.

Well, another milestone passed, she thought. *Everything had worked out fine with the craft week, and all had gone home happy. What more could one do? Nothing.*

She knew there was no point in wishing Max was with her. She had met Max a year ago when they came to Lindos for Tanya's card making class. He, a widower, and Ruth, a single lady of similar age, became firm friends, and had announced their engagement before the week was over. As Tanya and her aunt June wished to give up the little craft holiday business, Max and Ruth made plans to move to Rhodes and take over this small, but enjoyable, enterprise.

His sudden death, in England, had left Ruth devastated.

But she had commitments to the craft group, and Max had taken a ten-year lease on a spiti in Lindos. At least she still had her house in Stowe, had not burnt all her boats; and knowing that had made it easier to try and give this new life a chance.

Now, with the May craft week behind her, she had the rest of the summer to relax and enjoy what life on a Greek island had to offer. But, if she was going to achieve anything today, she had better get out of her dressing gown and put on some proper clothes.

Then the phone rang. 'Be with you in ten, put the kettle on'.

Phil Davenport begrudged paying three euros for an English newspaper. After all, it was printed in Athens each day, and came over on the ferry, so what justified that mark up? But this morning the headlines, on a stand outside the petrol station, caught his eye and he succumbed. 'Gang involved in diamond heist latest report'.

'It seems that many of those currently on remand for involvement with last years' safe deposit theft in London are seventy-year-old Pensioners'.

He had to smile. He pushed the newspaper into his rucksack and rode on from Kalathos to Lindos. He had a car, but given the choice, Phil preferred his motorbike. The scenery never ceased to amaze him, the hills covered in a slight morning mist, the sea, as still as a mill pond, and a stunning ice blue. White houses completed the picture and left you in no doubt that you were on a Greek island. He had rung Ruth to tell her he was on his way, an unwritten rule amongst the British 'expats' on Rhodes. Now he steered his motorbike carefully through the narrow lanes of Lindos. Just a small job to do today for a friend. The paper would keep.

****

If Ruth had wondered how she would fill the time once the craft group had gone home, then the reality was a bit of a shock. But, for a lady who had been busy all her life, quite a pleasant one. The first visitor with a mission was Phil. Although he had offered to come to the house when Ruth returned to Lindos, she had thanked him, but delayed the offer until the craft week was over, and the guests had left.

'Right, have you put the kettle on?' Phil asked with northern bluntness as he looked around the lounge.

'Now, where do you need more sockets putting in? One place is rather obvious as I can see that lamp sitting on the side table with an extension'. He continued to survey the little lounge. 'It does look nice with the sun shining in, but have you got thicker curtains, because in a few weeks you will need to shut that bit of sun out or you will roast alive. Sort them out and I will put them up when I come through again'. There was no discussion about it, which made her smile.

'I have not worked out what to do with the kitchen yet', she said as they sat with tea and digestives in the courtyard half an hour later.

'Well, unless you intend to buy something new with marble tops and oak doors then maybe I can help you out', he told her, his hand over his mouth covering a half-chewed biscuit.

'Chris has ordered a new kitchen from Italy, arriving in a couple of weeks. We were wondering what to do with the units we have now, except put them on the tip. So, if it is a few kitchen cupboards you need with a couple of wall ones for your plates and things, ours might do the job'.

Ruth laughed, 'That idea sounds brilliant, thank you. It never ceases to amaze me how often things just seem to work out right. Now what do I owe you for the work today', she asked.

'Just for the materials please sweetheart. I have the bill here somewhere. I guessed about four sockets, and the cable and that worked out right. We can add things to the kitchen when it is sorted'.

'But what about your time, that needs to be covered', Ruth asked, wishing to be fair to him for his help. 'No, just the materials, twenty-eight euros, count it as a welcome back gift if you like'. Ruth was most appreciative and accepted graciously.

She did wonder how the kitchen units would get from Kalathos to Lindos, but she was beginning to realize that everything could be arranged somehow, with a bit of help from fit and able younger friends.

****

And somehow, one day seemed to lead into another.

Tina, the young girl from Bournemouth, called in nearly every day. Ruth guessed that she was homesick, for all her brave talk about how exciting it was living on a Greek island and meeting so many new people at the Crazy Moon. 'And they come from all over the world, and they all speak English', she told Ruth.

Heather, who had been on the same craft course as Ruth, was now living in a caravan down the island, in the village of Asklipios. She often rang to say that she and Lucy were on their way back from a Lindos beach, and if Ruth was not busy …. And naturally Ruth was never too busy to entertain her young guests with a frappe and ice cream.

Ruth had now changed her morning walk and instead of going to Krana she went down to Pallas beach and along the narrow donkey path to the big beach.

Sometimes she turned up and past the small chapel in the field and then stopped for a coffee and chat with Rocos at Oasis. Sometimes she walked on to the Dolphin bar where she enjoyed a chat with Eric, or more correctly, Enrico. On other days, she went right along to the end of the big beach to Palestra, drinking her latte in the company of Nikos and Rosanna.

How she fitted in her trips to Rhodes to help Christian, Ken and Tony at the cemetery, was a bit of a mystery, but she did and was enjoying every minute of it. But today she was only going as far as the post office, sending a few letters back to Stowe, pay the electric bill and collect any post for herself.

She knew she had at least one letter as she had met Sheila in Sandra's shop and she had told Ruth. When your letters are in a shoebox on the counter everyone can see who has got post. A novel idea, but it worked in a village where not all the streets had names, and not all the houses had numbers.

Best of all it was a great place for bumping into people and stopping for a chat. In fact, there were times when the small space was full, but no one at the counter waiting to be served, just people stopping to gossip about something or nothing with their friends.

There was a letter from Merle, who not only kept an eye on Ruth's house in England but had also adopted her cat. It all seemed so far away, almost another planet, not just another country. So many people used emails now that those who wrote letters were rare, and usually people of a certain age. It was no surprise to find a missive from Margaret. Ruth retraced her steps to the spiti looking forward to reading her post.

Margaret had also been on that first craft holiday last year. She had visited Lindos for many years with her husband but returned last year for her granddaughter's wedding. Now widowed, and not wishing to join the younger family members on the beach, she had joined the craft group to pass the time till the wedding on the Saturday. She and Ruth became good friends, and as Margaret was a dab hand at Chinese painting, Ruth asked her to teach now she was organizing the event.

But it was the letter with a typed address that took Ruth's curiosity, and which she opened first.

Dear Ruth,

It is with great regret that I tell you I will not be able to help with the autumn craft week in Lindos. It has been an exciting and interesting experience, both the first classes and my week as a tutor for you. I feel sorry to let you down, but for family reasons I think it is for the best.

I am pleased to tell you that my craft group in the village has really taken off and I am quite busy with wedding stationery bookings. Thank you for everything and every good wish for your next holiday group,

> Yours sincerely   Mel

****

Mel had read and re-read the brief note before putting it into the envelope. She was concerned that it was not enough of an explanation, but what good would it do, telling Ruth how things had changed in the past few weeks. Her daughter Carol, unmarried but pregnant, had left home and was sharing a flat with her boyfriend. With the worry over Carol and the baby, there was no way Mel could deal with being away. She and Keith had never spoken about what had happened in Lindos, but both knew that it continued to hang over them, regardless of more pressing problems concerning their daughter.

*******.

Ruth was torn between her concern for Mel and her family, wondering what was wrong that had caused this change of heart, and her own predicament, finding a competent tutor for card making in the autumn. At least they had decided to run with cards in general, not specifically wedding stationery and it was not till October anyway.

If need be, I can just teach the card sessions myself. Having the right equipment is more important than experience, I am sure. Once a teacher, always a teacher, but I am certain there will be a solution, Ruth mused to herself.

Not for the first time, she wondered what had induced her to take the whole venture on. In her heart, she knew that had Max been there, decisions about the craft project would ultimately have been hers anyway. But at least she would have someone to talk it over with. And the bursary. What a lovely idea that seemed at the time, and it still was, she knew that. No way would she not run a free holiday for young people.

Things will work out. Leave it in God's hands.

****

LORD BERTRAM RAWLINS picked up the Times as he walked through to the balcony of the Melenos hotel for his breakfast.

Still making the front page, he thought. *And mostly pensioners? It seems I am not too late to start a new career!*

But nothing was further from his mind. He had done thirty-five years with the R.A.F. and that was enough, in his opinion, to merit a life of comparative idleness. And no one could fulfil that brief better than Bertie, as he preferred to be known. And today was Thursday, so a game of golf, and a light lunch. Then perhaps a swim, and a snooze on the beach. Back to Melenos for a shower and a whiskey or two. And one of the most enjoyable evenings of the week, dinner with Ruth at the spiti.

It was through Maxim that Bertie had been introduced to Ruth. He and Max had often served together in their time in the R.A.F. During the craft holiday Max had bumped into Bertie outside the Melenos Hotel. The Melenos was always Bertie's choice of residence.

It had fallen to Bertie to arrange Max's funeral in England. Now he and Ruth met quite regularly. An enjoyable friendship

He had been sneezing during the day, but he was sure that a couple of 'Jack Daniels' would ward off any symptoms of ill health. After all it was Thursday.

****

'Man flu', Ruth enquired with an unusual sarcastic tone to her voice.

'I don't know what you are talking about', Bertie replied. 'I thought you would be kind to a dumb animal'.

'Kind, yes, but you don't deserve my sympathy. If you are unwell, you stay home and get better. Yet you were out early this morning playing golf. Now sit down and in ten minutes supper will be ready'.

They had fallen into a sort of routine, having a home cooked meal on Thursday evenings in Ruth's little house. Then they would watch a film on DVD, and Bertie usually left at about eleven. Often it was later than that as over a nightcap they chatted about Max, and Ruth learnt more about the man she had intended to marry. She found it very healing to speak of their mutual friend to Bertie, rather than replying to the polite sympathy offered by strangers.

Ruth had not realized how close the friends had been. Not that Bertie dwelled on the bad times in Korea, but she was to learn of near-death experiences of the young pilot and his gunner. How, in later years, Max and Bertie had both been posted to Malta, enjoying comparatively comfortable office jobs and once again able to renew their friendship.

At other times Ruth and her guest talked of their home life as children, he from a relatively privileged background, a country estate in the south of England and she from an immigrant Irish family, her father coming to the midlands to work on the motorway construction. What they both had in common was a secure and loving background, but not without its problems.

Ruth had explained how difficult it had been to cope with the move to England, 'For a long time I thought our grandmother did not want us, and that was why we moved. My parents thought it was because I missed Grandma that I could not settle. Then at Christmas she came over to England and stayed for about a month. We had a few little chats, with Grandma telling me how much she missed us all, and that Daddy had to move as he needed the work. After that I was ok. about it all'.

On another evening Bertie told how, when sent to boarding school at nine years old, he thought it was because he was not wanted at home. He kept wondering what he had done to deserve being sent away. Then when he had a good end of year report his father told him how proud he was, that his little man had done so well, and that they were worried about him settling in, and if he had not, they would have brought him home. 'I wish they had taken me home. It took me a long time to get accustomed to being away from my family'.

Ruth did not feel the need to talk about her brother Francis or her daughter Ellen. Well, not yet, and Bertie did not talk about the girl he had been engaged to. Well, not yet.

But this evening Bertie had no sooner sat back in the armchair after supper than he fell asleep. Ruth pottered around in the kitchen for a while but on return to the lounge found him hot and flushed. She went into the spare bedroom, opened the second drawer, took out a pair of Max's pyjamas and his cotton dressing gown and laid them on the bed. When Bertie awoke an hour later, she had pulled down the blind and put on the fan.

'So sorry Ruth, what a bore I am this evening. I do feel rough. I had better go'.

'You are not going anywhere tonight, only as far as the bedroom', Ruth told him.

'Ruth dear, how could you make me such an offer when I am feeling so unwell?' he replied, his quick wit not deserting him even in his present state.

'The spare bedroom, with emphasis on the spare, and there are pyjamas on the bed and towels if you wish to shower, and cold 'Lemsip' in the glass next to the bed. Now go and get a good sleep and I hope you are better in the morning'.

Bertie was beginning to recognize the teacher's voice, which brooked no argument. He thought it best not to say good night in the usual Greek way for fear of passing on his infection. He regretted being as silly as to come to St. Raphael that evening and put Ruth in danger of catching his cold. And with that thought he went to the bathroom and not for the first time was pleased that he always carried a folding toothbrush.

Ruth knew that the throw away remark about the bedroom was exactly that, a throw away remark to lighten the atmosphere and his feeling of impotence the 'flu' had rendered in him. But Ruth found it strangely disturbing, and not in an unpleasant way. But as charming a companion that Bertie could be, she was not foolish enough to consider anything other than friendship with a man who had gone off cruising around the Greek islands with Claire only last summer. And obviously, they had kept in touch, even under the guise of stone cleaning his country estate.

What am I thinking of, silly old biddy, she told herself before she fell asleep.

She was awake early, intending to make tea and take a cup into Bertie. Then she saw the note on the kitchen table.

'Slept like a log, feel good this a.m. gone to get a change of clothes, thanks for last night, xx B'.

Oh well, that saves a discussion about the shower, Ruth thought, but had to admit she was looking forward to company for breakfast.

****

IT WAS A WEEK LATER when Phil's wife Chris rang Ruth.

'Is it ok if Phil drops by this morning to put the curtains up for you?', she asked. 'Also, the new kitchen is arriving on Saturday, and we thought it would be a good idea for you to come back up to the house with Phil and pick the units you need. There is no point in moving them from here and you then trying to get rid of the spare ones at some later date. Phil will measure it up when he gets down there, but it is up to you what you have'.

It was only yesterday, after breakfast, that Ruth was thinking about what she needed in the way of kitchen cupboards. On the envelope from the OTE office she had drawn up a sketch. Somewhere in the back of her mind she recalled that kitchen units were twenty-one or forty-two inches wide, 'but heaven knows what that is in centimetres', she had asked herself aloud. But in her sewing box was an old cloth tape with inches on one side and centimetres on the other, problem solved. If she had guessed right, she would be able to fit three cupboards on the long wall. She would keep the old Belfast sink and fit the lower units around it. But all this was conjecture as she had no idea what was being offered. One thing she did want, if possible was a plate draining unit above the sink, and as the sink was not under the window, this should not be a problem.

The house in Kalathos was not on either of the new estates but one of seven built on a rocky outcrop above Old Kalathos village. There they had settled down to the lifestyle they dreamed of when coming to Greece. Because of Phil's erratic hours in the Fire Service, they were used to leading independent lives, and this they continued to do. So, they avoided the major problem of retired couples in a foreign country, sitting aimlessly in bars, for want of something better to do. Both drove, rather than one not bothering to cope with driving 'on the wrong side'. Phil always managed to find a few jobs to supplement his pension, and ran a local gym, more for amusement than financial gain.

Together they organized a quiz night in the bar once a week in the winter. Twice a year he returned to England to visit his mother, then down to London to see their son. Joe had been at drama school when they first came to Rhodes and now had a successful career in West End theatre. Chris did the same, visiting her son first, then spend a week with her family in Essex. That way there was always someone at home to look after the house and feed the cat.

'This road gets nigh washed away in the winter', Phil explained to Ruth as they left the main road and started the steep climb to the old village of Kalathos. 'It's a bona fide public road, so should get repaired but it is left to us to fill in the holes where we can'. Ruth looked down at the riverbed running way below the narrow bridge and thought she would not want to be doing the journey on a wet winter's night.

The dominating building was the church, surrounded by a lovingly tended graveyard. Past this and on to an outcrop of stone that no Greek had considered building on in almost two thousand years of habitation. But now there stood a group of seven modern houses.

The view was amazing. There was a low walled garden at the front and a pool. From the lounge, you had an uninterrupted view, as glass doors ran the width of the room. Ruth imagined how beautiful it must be to sit there in the evening and see nothing but twinkling lights from the houses below and beyond that, the sea and sky.

Phil agreed with Ruth's guestimate, and suggested she take an extra unit for making shelves in the corners.

'Is there anyone else who might need a cupboard or two?', she asked.

'Not that I know of, why?'

'Well, if I am not depriving anyone of something they need, may I take them all?', Ruth suggested. 'There is nothing in the bathroom and what is surplus could well go in there'. Phil was pleased, as it would have been almost as much trouble getting rid of what was spare than dealing with the whole kitchen.

'Now, what do I owe you?', she asked

'Me? Nothing at all. You are doing me a favour. I will organize the lads to deliver, maybe Miles and

Graham, then you pay them'. 'But I must …', she started to say, but the only response she got was 'tea or coffee'?

****

PART 2

NIGEL ARRIVED IN LINDOS on a day tripper boat from Rhodes Town. Desperate for a swim, he had asked Heather if she would mind his backpack whilst he went into the sea.

'It is only that my passport is in there', he explained. 'Anything else, anyone is welcome to, if they need it'.

Later, over tea and ice cream at Scala, Heather told him she was not a tourist, but lived in a caravan down the island. When he asked about being able to camp on the site, she invited him to put his tent up in the field. He later offered to pay rent but, as he had already fixed the gate and mended the down pipe into the water butt, Heather refused. So, he weeded and watered the large vegetable patch in return. He had plans to move off down to Prasonissi, where many young people were camping on the sand dunes. Starting a summer ministry would give his Greek holiday some meaning.

Besides an excuse for a day out, Heather wanted to take Nigel into the Light House restaurant and introduce him to Asimeni. It was only a short drive through the barren landscape, recently laid waste by a forest fire, to the end of the island where the two seas meet.

Heather stopped the car on the rise of the hill to allow Nigel to take in the view. The grass was sparse, but wild daisies and anemones covered the rocky ground. They looked down on a long beach with the sea on both sides. At the far end, where the beach narrowed to barely a meter of sand, the outcrop known as Green Island, or Prasonissi in Greek, rose out of the sea. Back in the car they drove down towards the beach as far as the tarmac road would allow.

'Let's go and get a coffee first', Heather suggested, and with Lucy perched high on Nigel's shoulders they walked down to the Light House restaurant.

Nigel was disappointed. 'I thought there would be more tents around, you know, back packers camping overnight', he said.

'Oh, but there are', Heather explained. 'The tents are around the corner out of the wind. No one wants to see their belongings sailing off to sea'.

He laughed at himself. 'Ye of little faith', he thought.

At that moment, when there was a break from serving lunch to a coach full of Danish tourists, Asimeni came over to chat.

After the friends had warmly greeted each other, Heather introduced Nigel. She explained, 'Nigel is from Canada. He is going to camp down here all summer and run a Christian ministry for the young people'.

'You will need a room to keep your things and take a shower. Showering on the beach is o.k. for a week but longer than that is not comfortable', Asimeni suggested. Nigel thanked her for the offer but explained that he was on a budget.

'Well, I was thinking that our studios were not always full, so you are welcome to make use of a room. Let's say if we get a high demand for accommodation, I will tell you'. It was an offer he could not refuse and accepted gracefully.

'I am quite a useful handyman, so please ask me if there is anything I can do in return', he told her, and then went to get his kit from the car. He could not believe his good fortune. Certainly, to have a space to return to in the heat of the day was sheer luxury in his opinion.

After they paddled in the sea and ate ice cream and apple pie, he waved goodbye to Heather and Lucy. That evening Nigel slept in the studio, as Asimeni had suggested. The following morning, he looked for a spot to pitch his tent. He had decided to give himself a few days, to just wander around and talk to people. Then, he would distribute his leaflets inviting those who wished to join his campfire in the evenings. He thanked God for his good fortune and vowed to give all he could to his ministerial work in the next few months.

****

Now Heather was alone again, as her employers were still in England, life in the small Greek village had changed. No trips to the school, no typing and filing of receipts. She had nothing to do all day but look after Lucy, feed the cat and head for the beach. Yes, it was a bit lonely at times, but of course there were always tourist to talk to.

'You live here? Wow, lucky you', was the usual comment when asked was her holiday for one week or two. And Heather would repeatedly explain how she, a young single mum from Edinburgh, ended up living on a Greek island.

There were times when she wondered about this herself. It was not as though she had this ambition to move away from her beloved Edinburgh, or even from her adopted Manchester.

When her marriage went 'on the rocks', she had gone up north to stay with her parents. But the house in Dalkeith, where they now lived, had never been her home, and nothing like the cottage in Dean Village where she had spent her childhood.

Aware that Heather was still unsettled, almost a year after the break-up of her marriage, her mother suggested she took a holiday, and her parents would look after the two-year-old, Lucy. Not wishing to be on the beach all day, or in a restaurant in the evenings on her own, Heather had booked into the craft group. During that week she met Trish and her husband, an English couple, trying to start a business and ferry their children to school in Lindos each day, Heather was offered the job of 'girl Friday' and accepted.

And the rest is history. Heather and Lucy still have their mobile home, and the use of the car. But, as her employers had explained, they would not be able to pay Heather whilst they were away. That was not a problem, particularly as Heather now had three non-Greek children coming to the caravan twice a week for extra maths lessons. Heather found it hard to believe that she had now been living in Asklipios for almost a year.

****

When her dad Skyped for a chat, she suggested that he and her mother came over. After all, the main house was empty for a few weeks, as Tim had not bothered to sublet it until later in the summer. Ken was more than pleased with the idea, but her mother was less keen, already planning to go to Southport with her youngest daughter and her two boys.

So Ken decided to make the trip on his own, much to the surprise of the rest of the family. He wanted to assure himself that everything was well with Heather and Lucy. He knew Heather would not ask for help but if there was anything they needed, where a little cash injection would make a difference, he would find it for them.

****

The journey was not as difficult as he expected. He flew direct from Glasgow to Rhodes. Granted he arrived at midnight, but to get there without any fuss, he could not believe his luck. And it was not expensive, and as he had slept on the plane, he could sit at the airport until there was a bus into the town.

By the time he had collected his case and found a bathroom it was half past five, Greek time. The airport was already busy, so no problem finding an English- speaking rep to direct him to the bus stop. He hesitated for a moment, not knowing how to ask for the bus station in Greek, but to his surprise, when the lad in front of him just asked in English, the driver did not blink. 'That is one euro twenty cents please?' was the immediate reply, not a problem.

Ken thought he would be tired, but the adrenalin rushed through his body as the bus left the airport and sped towards the capital. Past narrow streets and shopping precincts, with occasional glimpses of the sea. Then a long stretch of coastline, with massive white hotels on the inland side of the road. Once away from the coast, Ken smiled as the bus stopped outside Marks and Spencer. Two minutes later they turned into the bus station.

Heather had told Ken to take a bus to Archangelos. There would be plenty of cafes there, and she would come and collect him. He was to ring her as soon as he was on the bus. He was pleased he was travelling alone. No fuss if things did not work out as planned, so he felt relaxed about the whole strange experience.

Ken did not feel tired at all, although he knew it was the adrenalin. He would crash as soon as he was in the caravan, but he would deal with that when the time came. He heard the man in the ticket office talking on his phone, and in English. That was a relief.

'Excuse me, what time will the bus get into Archangelos', he asked. 'I have been travelling all night', he explained, 'and I need to set my alarm'.

The man smiled as he gave Ken his change. 'Ask the driver, sit near the front and he will call you when you get there'. Ken was not sure what to make of this, surely the man cannot remember everyone? But then logic set in, and he realized that most other passengers knew where to get off and when. Once in the bus, an elderly man sat beside him.

'What a lovely morning', he addressed Ken with an upper crust English accent you could cut with a knife. 'Are you travelling far?' Once Ken had got over the surprise of being on a bus in Greece and being spoken to in English, he told him.

'To visit my daughter in Asklipios, but she said to get off the bus in Archangelos and she will collect me from there'.

'A wise move, you could be all day in and out the villages, and you will have breakfast finished long before the bus gets that far. Is this your first visit to Rhodes?' he asked.

Ken explained about Heather, and her job, and the caravan in a village up in the mountains. What another surprise when Bertie told Ken he had met his daughter on several occasions, and what a lovely young lady she was. He explained how he knew the lady that now runs the craft group and had joined them for supper one evening. Bertie pointed out the villages they went past, and the journey sped by. But eventually sleep caught up with Ken and the next thing he was getting a gentle tap on his shoulder.

'We are coming into Archangelos now, I wish you a very enjoyable visit'. They shook hands as Bertie moved from the seat to let Ken get out. Then the driver called out 'Archangelos, main stop. This is your stop', and he was looking in the mirror to see if Ken was making a move. You are supposed to get off by the back door, but the bus was not full, so the driver did not insist, and as Ken passed him, he slipped a five euro note onto the dashboard.

True to her word, Heather was waiting with an excited Lucy jumping up and down beside her. And by half past nine that morning he was sitting in the caravan with a coffee.

'When the family were here it was a bit of a marathon', Heather explained. 'But without Tim and Trish I would not be in Greece anyway', she told her dad. 'After all we have a caravan to live in, the car to drive, and I am not touching the maintenance money Dave pays into the bank for Lucy'. So, his mind at rest he could sit back and enjoy his holiday.

The most important thing for him was spending quality time with his favourite daughter and seeing how relaxed and happy she was. The drive down through the mountains to the beach, playing in the sand with Lucy, being there to pick her up when a wave frightened her, all that was a bonus. Somehow, he had not imagined Greece to be like this. Certainly, the days were hot, but with the constant breeze it was very pleasant. And walking down over the fields full of margarites, clumps of thyme and the occasional wild orchid! All a reminder of his childhood home in Strathpeffer, only the heather was missing.

****

Ken's morning walk to the shop included a stop at Sylvia's café. There he ordered a 'Nescafe', as he had not yet acquired a taste for the strong black coffee the other men were drinking. Ken was surprised to find that, even in this small mountain village of Asklipios, most people spoke English. And even more surprised to find they did so with an Australian accent. One particularly quiet morning Eleni's father, Vasilis, explained this to Ken.

'There have been Sklipenious people in Australia since 1912. So, when my friend and I set out in 1953 we felt that we had family to go to. To be honest everyone from the village was related in those days, for that is how it was. And in Brisbane, Tom and Rigopoula, who had been in Australia since 1924, always found room in their home for newly arrived emigrants. We stayed with them until we found a room for ourselves'.

'A tough decision for a young man to make in those days', Ken observed.

Vasilis smiled. 'Once you get the idea in your head you have to follow it through. We all had a small inheritance from our grandparents, that was how it was in those times, one generation sacrificed everything to give the young people a chance. And things were bad in Greece in the fifties. Yes, the war was over in Europe, but Greece had her own problems'.

Vasilis explained how he and his friend journeyed for weeks by boat, most of the time uncertain when the next ship, or the next meal would come. 'There was no ten-pound assisted travel like the British government had for your countrymen'.

'But you struck lucky then and got work', Ken asked the elderly man. Vasilis sighed and then smiled. 'Work', he repeated, his mind's eye searching back for the memories.

'At first there was no work. We often walked all day, from farm to farm looking to be taken on. Sometimes we got lost, not sure of the way back to town, but then if we were lucky a truck would come by and lift us back to Brisbane. The only English words we knew was 'job?' or 'no job'. I remember we got a few days' work shovelling stones on a mountain. And I never did get paid, no I never got paid', he recalled, shaking his head.

Then he laughed at the memory, his eyes smiling as he remembered those days so many years ago.

'By the end of the second day our hands were all blistered. How I cried and prayed to God to take me home to Greece'. He looked down at his hands as though the blisters could still be felt.

'So how did you not get your money if you had worked for it, and worked hard at that? It does not seem fair', Ken told him.

'I never did get paid because next day I was told of another job and never went back digging stones. The new job was in Ipswich. I had to go on a train and was sick that I would not remember the English letters for 'Ipswich'. But there were young soldiers on the train, and they told me the right station'.

Ken had to admit it was something he had not considered, that just as he could not read the Greek alphabet today, Vasilis and his friend, when leaving Greece, could not read the English script, let alone speak the language.

'I got the job in Ipswich and stayed there seven years. I worked hard and learnt all I could. I became a good carpenter and managed to save some money. I set up my own workshop. I did not look back'.

The older man stood up to leave and turning to Ken added 'We must talk again; it was not all bad times. We had some good fortune, and we could feed and raise a family. Yes, we were so fortunate', and still with his mind in the past Vasilis wandered back down the village to his simple but comfortable home. His home in the same village he left all those years ago.

It was Eleni, Vasilis' daughter, who took up her parents' story when she visited Heather and Ken at the caravan one afternoon.

'My mother Irene and my father had been good friends since school days. Once Dad was sure of a regular job, and had some money saved, he sent for Mum to come and join him in Brisbane. There was actually a scheme set up by the Queen of Greece for women to join their prospective husbands abroad, but my grandfather was able to pay for my mother himself'.

'What a different world it was then, to wave goodbye to your family, not knowing if you would ever see them again. No Skype or internet, no hopping on a plane for a few days' holiday. It was the same for families leaving the highlands except they all had a common language', Ken told Eleni.

'When did you first come to Rhodes?' Heather asked.

'I was twelve when we came back for a holiday, Mum, Dad and my brothers Emanuel and Stergos. I loved Greece, and once I was working, and had money saved, I came back here several times. Then I met my husband and returned for good, except to go to Australia to visit my parents'.

Eleni told them her mother and father returned to Asklipios five years ago, and her mother had died last year.

Just before Ken returned home to Scotland he was chatting again with Vasilis, and the conversation turned to the Syrian refugee crisis.

'How can we turn them away?' Vasilis asked. 'Greek people have gone to every corner of the earth to work, to build a new life for their family. And everywhere you wait for the good will of strangers, to give you a room, to give you work, to make you welcome. And how can you not bring women and children from the sea?' he shook his head in disbelief that anyone should be asked to do such a thing.

'I feel sorry for these migrants today', the elderly man told Ken. 'At least we had a chance of work years ago, but now….', and his voice trailed off, his mind in the past but his heart reaching out to others and a history repeating itself.

****

Ken had enjoyed the holiday with Heather and his little granddaughter. It had been a great experience, learning the history of the place, and getting to know the lovely local people, and some of Heather's expat friends. Not the normal two weeks by the sea, but it left a deep impression on him. On a trip into Lindos he had met Ruth and felt even more at ease, leaving his daughter and granddaughter in such good hands. He thought about his emotional goodbye to Heather and the adorable Lucy. No matter what plans the rest of the family might have, he would return to Rhodes in the Autumn.

****

Ruth had rung Bertie to say that she would enjoy his company on Thursday if he had nothing else planned.

Late that Thursday evening, after dinner, with their usual nightcap in hand, Bertie asked Ruth if she enjoyed dancing.

'Well, there is dancing, and dancing', she replied.

'Oh, ordinary dancing, ballroom I expect you would call it'.

'Absolutely love to dance but am rather out of practice these days. Though I expect it is a bit like riding a bike, you never really forget'.

'The thing is, I have always enjoyed going to dances in the past, but as you say, one gets a bit out of practice. It is just that I met up with an American Greek chap at a friend's house last time I was up in Rhodes. He runs dance classes a couple of times a week. Very informal'.

'Oh, did you meet Stathis?' Ruth asked with a smile. Well, it was a small island, and the number of American Greeks organising dance classes would be few and far between.

'You know him? What a charming man. He was visiting Thanasis, in the Old Town, when I dropped by for a chat. Thanasis knows I am looking for a place up there and had heard of one near him. It is a good area, but the rooms were quite small, and I do like some space'.

'I was with Stathis and his friends, Andonis and Zenia, at the May Day celebrations in St. Paul's bay. We had a lovely afternoon. Naturally, it was all Greek dancing. I would have been completely completely lost, except that they were all such good dancers, and just carried me along'.

This was more than Bertie bargained for when he had opened the conversation. He could do a reasonable jive, and loved both the 'old time', and the ordinary form of waltz, but that was his limit.

'Oh, I think this is just a beginner's class, though some are serious students, it is a fun evening I understand.

'Yes, I attended some classes and found it most enjoyable. The experienced dancers help others, which gives such a lovely atmosphere. The problem is getting back to Lindos, as buses go to Archangelos at that time in the evening'.

Bertie had already enquired, and decided the best plan was to go on the bus, then on the way home, get a taxi from Archangelos.

'We could go a few times and see how we get on, it would be a bit of fun, and good exercise', he suggested. And plans were made for the next Tuesday evening, which was usually their day for just doing their own thing, particularly after a late Monday night at Medeast.

Eustathios Stratis had always loved Greece since he and his sister came on holiday after finishing college. They travelled from Boston to Athens first and had taken in all the historical sights. Then on through the islands, until they came to Rhodes, where they stayed for three months.

And for Stathis, there was no going back. Having dual nationality, he soon secured a teaching post at the university. His brief was to train teachers on how to teach dance and movement to young children.

When Ruth had been to the classes before, Stathis had met her at the bus station Then Michael Gaunt, a retired Englishman, who had lived in the Old Town for more than twenty years, had escorted her back to the bus terminal. So, she was not sure if she could find the way herself. It was behind the Catholic church of Santa Maria, sort of inland from the far end of

Mandraki harbour. Bertie said you could get there easier from Johnny's bar. Once he got there, he would know the way. It did not matter, it was a lovely afternoon, and they left Lindos in plenty of time.

Ruth thought the walk would be a lovely warm up exercise. At least she had kept her sandals on and carried her heeled dance shoes in her shoulder bag. Eventually they came to the hall, but if anyone had asked how they got there, neither would have been able to give a cohesive answer.

'I think we should go back via Mandraki', Bertie suggested. Ruth just smiled. If there was one thing any man disliked, it was being given directions by a woman. Which was why she had let Bertie choose their route to the hall in the first place.

Stathis was talking with an elderly couple, and it was a relief for Bertie to see that the students were not all young.

It was Andonis who recognized Ruth first, giving a shout of 'Kalispera', and came towards her with open arms, and the customary kiss on both cheeks. Introductions made, the men chatted, as did Zenia and Ruth. The ice had been broken, not that neither Bertie nor Ruth were shrinking violets, but it is nice to be recognized when you walk into a group of people.

Then a squeal of delight came from across the room. It was Eleni from Asklipios. She rushed over to say hello. 'I work in town for three days a week', she explained. 'So, I stay up here for two nights each week.

Stathis clapped his hands and drew the class to order.

'As many of you know, I prefer to use the stage. The floor is sprung, and having a slightly damaged knee, it is better for all of us than the solid floor of the main hall. So, if you would like to find a space up there, looking out towards me, we will start with a warm-up exercise'.

Bertie threw Ruth a glance, as if they had not just done an hour's exercise! She shrugged her shoulders and smiled back. The music was on, and the class began. It was quite relaxing, and included some stretching, but nothing too strenuous.

'Now, I would like everyone to learn the beat and basic steps for the foxtrot this evening. Please form lines at the right-hand end of the stage'.

This caused a moment of confusion, as to which end is the right-hand end of a stage? But some seemed certain which way to go, and the lines were formed. Bertie had automatically gone to the back as he was quite used to being given this position due to his height. Ruth found herself in the middle, so was happy with that. There was no music, Stathis called out the slow, slow, quick, quick, slow rhythm. And one row at a time, they walked to the opposite end of the stage.

Ruth wanted to giggle. She had not been in this type of class since a child. Even when she had attended before, they had gone straight into partner hold, and danced the waltz.

'Now, ladies, you, naturally, will be walking backwards.'

He caught Ruth's hand and before she had a chance to protest, they were demonstrating the step.

'It is only walking to the beat of the music, but many people find this the most difficult of the ballroom dances to master', Stathis told the group. 'Find your partners please and we will try with music. Zenia and Andonis, if you do not mind splitting up for the moment and take Ruth and Bertrum please'.

Not often Bertie got his full name these days, must be on a charge or something he reflected, with a wry smile. Stathis moved amongst the group, showing some how to hold their partners more correctly, but mostly praising his assorted students for their efforts.

The music stopped and there was a visible sigh of relief. They had mastered the first steps of a new dance. This was followed by a waltz, danced with a partner in hold, and everyone was able to do this with a reasonable measure of success. After a short break, Stathis changed the music to a Greek dance tune.

'Now those of you who know this dance, please join in. Everyone else sit down, listen to the beat of the music, and watch'. The group, arms stretched across each other's shoulders, began the slow rhythmic steps around the stage. The music began to get faster, and faster. Both Ruth and Bertie were quite relieved that they could legitimately sit out.

Bertie checked his watch, they needed to leave soon, to catch the last bus. They quietly changed their shoes, and waved goodbye to everyone, amidst various calls of 'see you on Friday'. It was not difficult to find the road down to Mandraki, and walk briskly along the sea front, enjoying the cool evening breeze. Just getting to the bus station on time they ran, buying their tickets on the bus. Ruth and Bertie sank, exhausted, into a seat about halfway down the aisle. They felt relaxed and happy, and both agreed it was one of the most enjoyable evenings of the summer.

Would they go again on Friday? Well, they would talk about it over supper at the spiti on Thursday night. The steady rhythm of the bus as it travelled in the dark soon had them dozing off. Soon they were in Archangelos.

****

If you were to ask Bertie or Ruth when their relationship changed, neither would be able to answer. But change it did. Somehow a kiss when they met, which might be the normal Greek custom, was delivered with his hands on her shoulders, not a handshake. She threw the tea towel at him, telling him to wipe the dishes whilst she made the coffee, and he threw it back saying he was making the coffee, and in Greece the dishes dry themselves, which caused a fit of laughter. And when he left her in the evenings the hug was longer than need be for friends to say goodnight. And sometimes he used the word 'darling' when saying goodnight on the phone.

That morning he had rung to ask Ruth if she was free to go to Medeast. He did not want to presume anything.

'Oh, that will be lovely, and it is so warm in the evenings now. I know I could go there at any time, but old habits die hard, and it still seems odd to walk into a restaurant unaccompanied'.

And as it was such a warm evening Ruth wore her turquoise sun dress, and matching sandals. Her hair, now a long bob, she turned under with the hair dryer. It was many years since she had worn this style, and it did flatter her.

Walking down the steps to the dining area was always exciting. Anticipating the view, then seeing the twinkling lights of the village, and beyond the dark blue sea.

The meal they chose, steak with pepper sauce, was as flavoursome as it always was, and on that Monday night, they stayed later than usual. Manolis had friends over from Athens and Bertie and Ruth had been invited to join them. Now, as they walked home, they were laughing and chatting in whispers along the darkened street, and Ruth was surprised to find they had not taken the usual turning back to her spiti but had walked up the hill and were now outside Melenos.

'Where are we going?' Ruth whispered, as they went past the hotel and up a small path. 'Somewhere special', he told her. 'Just come with me, you won't get lost', he said. The last few steps were quite steep, and it was almost dark. Ruth hung on to his arm to make sure she did not trip and fall.

They finally gained the little plateau outside a small church and turned to look across the expanse of the bay beneath them. Lights twinkled from the hotel and strung out past the school and down to the village.

There was no moonlight, just a velvet darkness and a Colbert blue sea as still as the night. They stood there quietly, looking out at the sea and stars.

'Don't go home Ruth', he said quietly. She did not reply.

'Don't go home tonight Ruth but come with me. Have a nightcap on the balcony and see where we go from there?'

Ruth moved away and sat on the wall. She found the last of her cigarettes and a lighter. Bertie stood in silence watching a small boat skim across the water, barely visible on the moonless sea. Then he went to the top of the path as if he was undecided what to say or do. He spoke without turning towards her.

'Ruth, would you stay with me tonight? Do you think it can happen for us?' he asked in a voice that was barely a whisper. He continued to gaze out to sea. The silence seemed to last forever then he turned towards Ruth and took the few strides to sit on the stone wall beside her.

Ruth still did not answer but raised her face to his, only managing to bury her head in his chest.

'I just want to kiss you, to tell you what I cannot say'.

'Do you now? And do I want to hear these unspoken words, or will they make me cry?' he asked. They started to laugh and relax for the moment.

Now the laughter stopped, and tears came into her eyes. His arms went around her and inclining his head, he kissed her hair. 'And what were you going to say? Please tell me?'

'I can't say that I want you to hold me. The words will not come. Just accept that I am here'. He released her from the embrace and looked directly into her face.

'Ruth, I will never ask you to say or do anything that you cannot do with a full heart. It makes perfect sense, you with me. We want the same things for what is left of our lives. Friendship, laughter, and belonging to each other in a special way', he added in a solemn tone she had not heard from Bertie before. Holding her hand, he moved and standing, pulled her gently towards him.

'There must be no regrets and no promises. Just being honest with each other that is all. Now tell me what it was you wanted to say, or have you changed your mind?' he asked Ruth.

She took a deep breath and in hushed tones began.

'Sorry my hearing is not as good as it used to be, would you mind saying that again?'

They laughed and kept putting their fingers to their lips and saying 'Shush'. When suitably in control some few minutes later they took the steps down to Melenos.

They did not go out onto the balcony but into the spacious lounge area of the suite. Bertie poured Ruth a whisky and American adding just a little ice. He went towards the bathroom, emerging with a large white fluffy dressing gown.

'I think this will be fine for you. Just give me a few minutes and the bathroom will be all yours', he said, giving her a quick kiss on the cheek.

Ruth sat in silence except for the sound of the shower splashing. She was calm and happy and realized that this is what she had thought about for these past few months.

The studio was quite lavish. The sleeping area was draped, with a large tapestry hanging on the wall behind. To one side, on another level, was an expansive daybed, with deep cushions, also a comfy sofa. The coffee table was dark oak and carved. The song from Camelot went through her head. *'I wonder what the peasants are doing tonight'. Yes, I wonder,* she thought.

Ruth had loved Max, a gentle, kind, and appropriate love for a lady in her sixtieth years. But her joy of being with Bertie was different. Totally different, and she knew that one did not exclude the other. Life with Bertie would not be less or more, but different.

Eventually the Honourable Bertrum Rawlins emerged from the shower with no more apparel than he had emerged into the world with some seventy years before.

'All yours now, shall I take your glass? Would you like a refill? Ruth shook her head and clutching the dressing gown went to shower.

Certainly different she thought to herself.

Yes, different from the loving, but chaste, relationship she had shared with Max, even after they were engaged.

The shower was spacious, the tiles and the glass door gleaming. She found a fresh flannel left for her on top of two thick white towels. She placed her sundress and briefs on the hooks behind the door. There were little phials of shampoo and one of shower cream on a glass shelf. Ruth chose a shampoo and once she had the water running washed and rinsed her hair. There was enough in the bottle to lather her body and she took her time. It was a long time since she had spent so long just having a shower.

But delay as much as she could, eventually Ruth stepped out of the shower and wrapped a towel around her.

At last she decided, and in another minute, was walking back into the apartment lounge. The white dressing gown was over her arm ... and she was wearing her turquoise sundress.

Bertie closed the book he was pretending to read. He took the dressing gown from her as he kissed her cheek.

'Now sweet lady, what can I get you to drink?'

Bertie had dressed in a beige shirt and the khaki shorts he always wore when lounging around. It occurred to Ruth that maybe he had guessed how the evening would resolve. 'Oh, I don't think I had quite finished the last one', she said looking around for the glass.

'No, but I did, just in case I needed some Dutch courage. So, shall we start again. What would you like to drink?' Bertie asked her as he held her in a gentle hug and kissed the top of her head.

'Then I will walk you home in the moonlight', he said in a low, soft voice.

'Bertie, I'm sorry', Ruth started to offer some explanation.

'Why? I am not. It is not the first time a girl has turned me down'. He stepped back from her, his head to one side. 'Not that it gets any easier, when my ego gets a basting', he pretended to look sad, then smiled.

He took her hands and gave her a long steady gaze, which she returned. 'Ruth, I am not going anywhere. Well only from Rhodes to England and back now and again. We can jog along, best of friends, just as we have been since Max died. Nothing has changed my dear girl. I hope you feel the same?'.

'What happened to that drink you were getting me?' Ruth asked by way of reply. 'And this is a five-star establishment, I will complain to the manager, the service is non-existent'.

They hugged again, a joyful bear hug.

The drinks poured, they walked out onto the balcony and sat on the comfy swing chair. There was no moon. Many of the village lights were now off, giving a feeling of velvet darkness.

How long they sat there for Ruth had no idea. They did not talk, there was no need, not between friends. Bertie had reached for her hand and was gently touching each finger in turn, just softly, so softly you would hardly notice. But Ruth did notice. She felt her body relaxing.

What if?

She put her glass down on the onyx side table, she stood and took Bertie's glass from him and placed it on the table.

'There is no moonlight, so maybe we had better wait till morning', she suggested quietly. He reached for her hand and bringing her closer to him, put a kiss on her fingertips.

'You could be right, and I would not risk you falling on the rocks. Morning would be a better idea'.

'And I am rather tired. Is there somewhere we could rest?'

'Yes, come with me, you can share my bed if you wish'.

'Oh, may I, how kind'.

****

PART 3

CHILHAM VILLAGE was as well preserved and protected as Lindos, and nearby Canterbury had a history that was more than a match for Rhodes town. Perhaps that was why Bertie felt a certain affinity with Rhodes, having spent so much of his youth in the shadow of a medieval castle, albeit in the Kent countryside.

He had picked up his car from a friend near Heathrow, and done what he enjoyed most about returning home, driven down the M 2 motorway, past familiar towns, until, before reaching Canterbury, he turned off towards Chilham.

And what better time of the year than now, with cherry trees still in bloom, and everywhere fresh from the late spring rain.

His parents had lived nearer to Dover, but he spent much of the school holidays in Chilham. And it was with the untimely death of his cousin, that Bertie had inherited the Grange.

But there was no way he wished to, or could afford to, give up his R.A.F. career to run a farm. As soon as he was legally able to do so, he signed the whole caboose over to his nephew Marcus. However, because of some ancient title deed, his signature was still required on some transactions.

Once he had settled into his own apartment on the first evening back, he was pleased to see that Claire was as much a part of the furniture and fittings as Marcus and the children were. Nothing could have delighted him more. He was devastated when his nephew's wife had died in that car crash, and Marcus was not only widowed, but left alone to bring up two lively children. Though Bertie knew that having the children had saved Marcus from total despair.

But Claire was the first person who seemed to move easily about the Grange without Marcus backing away from female company. Naturally, it was business, or was it?

From the business side of things, Claire's influence was certainly a breath of fresh air. She had started using the holiday let cottages as accommodation for the stone cleaning students.

The six- week course had been successful, and Reading University had booked for the next three years. Also, one of the tutors, more interested in historic buildings in general than just stone cleaning, had suggested an adult course following the development of the country house, as there were so many examples to be found within easy walking distance of the Grange. 'Particularly if you include supper at the 15th century Woolpack every evening', he added.

Maybe the time lapse was right for Marcus to move forward, and the children old enough to accept someone new into their lives, someone they obviously felt comfortable with, and they seemed comfortable with Claire. But then she did not try to mother them or be more than their friend. Perhaps it was just wishful thinking on Bertie's part. He certainly had more on his mind at that moment, as for once it was not just a casual return to Chilham.

Almost two years ago Marcus had received an offer from a French champagne company. They, and their wine merchant business partners, had purchased almost forty hectares of land on the edge of Chilham and they wished to acquire the small area that was Partridge Farm. Historically, it had never been part of the original Chilham Grange estate, only added on in the 17th century. The small farm had always been rented out and now lay fallow since the last elderly tenant had died, as none of his family wished to continue the lease.

Naturally, Marcus deferred to his uncle over the matter, though Bertie assured the younger man that the decision was his. The offer was more than generous, particularly as they did not want the cottages that went with the farm, or the small barn that the last tenant had used as a garage. Marcus decided to go ahead, it would relieve him of some tax duties, and make a cushion against anything that Brexit might bring. As it happened the legalities did need Bertie's signature, but that done, the sale went ahead. Bertie had added the proviso of a case of sparkling wine every year, once the vineyard was in production. Well why not? Even though it would be six years before he would reap the benefits of that part of the deal.

As for Bertie, he was more than happy with his own income from his RAF pension, with a small portfolio of shares, and some savings, for any extras.

This week Pierre-Emmanuel from the Champagne Taittinger estate in Reims was in Chilham to plant the first vines. The wine they intended to produce would be called Domain Evremond, named for the gentleman who first introduced champagne to the court of Charles the second.

Planting the first vines might have been a symbolic gesture, but the champagne flowing that evening at the Woolpack, was anything but symbolic. Not that Terry and Nicki were not used to posh parties at their establishment, but that evening was something special. And Marcus had brought Claire along to share it with him.

Bertie stayed on for another two weeks in his spacious apartment, enjoying being back in the atmosphere of antique furniture and a familiar lifestyle. He walked the land, and chatted to people in the pub. The county of Kent, in late spring, early summer, was a beautiful sight, with new grass and blossom on the apple and cherry trees. No wonder it was known as the garden of England.

Did he really have to live in Greece to be in a medieval setting? No, it was all here in this corner of his own country. Perhaps, for the first time since he had inherited the Grange, he began to feel that it could be home.

The evening before he returned to Rhodes, he was at the Woolpack again, only this time it was at the invitation of Marcus and Claire. It was an early supper, as the children were to be there as well. And to Bertie's surprise Claire's mother, Leila, and her aunt arrived. Quite a family gathering. And that is what it was, a family gathering, for after the meal Claire and Marcus announced their engagement.

****

PART 4

Simon Goodman closed the front door to his guest house in the seaside town of Folkestone. Well, it was not really his, but he had been managing it for so long he thought of it as his own.

You could say that Simon Goodman was a small-time crook.

You could, but you would be wrong, as Simon had never committed a crime, large or small. Though, strange but true, he does have a criminal record and he has done time. Big time. And the man he took the rap for has never forgotten it.

Old Geoff Marsham would have gone down for quite a long stretch thirty years ago, but he did not as Simon did it for him.

Everyone knew it was not Sy, but as he would not enter a 'not guilty' plea no one was going to argue. It suited the police just as much as it did Geoff. One less on the statistics, and they argued amongst themselves, if he had not done this job, then there were probably quite a few that he had done and got away with.

They were wrong. But Simon did not care at that moment. He had left home in Devon at fourteen and had only just managed to keep his head above water in London. He never found a job he liked or a boss who encouraged him. He was always the youngest in any flat share and was fed up with cooking and cleaning for everyone else. In a way, he was already in prison. What could be worse?

Geoff Marsham put the word in the right ears that Simon was his man and was to be treated accordingly. As for the prison staff, they quite liked the lad, always cheerful, cheeky without overstepping the mark, and quite soon, if he kept on the way he was going, the eight years he got would be commuted to four. And there was the open prison on the Isle of Sheppey and with luck he could be there in twelve months!

Geoff had plans for Simon. Not big plans that might put him inside again, but a nice little earner. Something he had been considering for quite a time, but he had never met the right person to put his trust in. Now there was this young man, not really part of the London scene, and as Geoff did not have a son, then this lad was the next best thing.

Not long after Simon's release Geoff set him up in a select B and B in Folkestone. It was his to run how he wished, always keeping one room vacant for special guests that Geoff would send from time to time. Obviously, there were parcels arriving quite regularly, but that was hardly a chore. Sy made a phone call and next day a courier arrived to pick up the package and Geoff rang to say it had arrived. As easy as that. And the lad made a good little business, with many returning clients, and Simon never asked about the special guests. Never.

Within a couple of years, he met Stella and with the arrival of two children life was complete. Once the kids were old enough, Stella returned to her job as a nurse. So, most days Simon was a full-time dad, finding it easy to fit in collecting the kids from school whilst still running his guest house. In the summer months they moved into a mobile home parked in the garden. This way, they always had room for extra guests.

Many of the customers were returning year after year, and even stretching the season into October now they had retired.

Eventually, Geoff, considering his luck might run out, gave up his criminal contacts in London and took the special room for himself.

Sometimes he would ask Simon to drive him up to the 'smoke' for an evening with old pals, but more often, these days, to attend a funeral.

But life moves on, and Simon was on his own now, except for old Geoff. Stella had left him, gone off with some bloke she had met at work, and the girls were now living in a flat of their own up in Dagenham.

Simon was always busy with the guest house. In the winter, he put up bunk beds, and rented out the rooms to job seekers, young unemployed lads. He would not have any drugs on the premises or too much drink and ensured they had good food. After all, he had been there and bought the tee shirt. But each year, just before Easter, he kicked them out, painted the rooms to get rid of the smell of fags, and had everything ready for his summer clientele. And the money was rolling in nice and steady, no problem.

Geoff was not always in the best of moods these days. Seemed preoccupied even when they sat and watched 'match of the day' on the big telly in the guests' lounge.

It was on the six o'clock news.

'Three blokes going down for that diamond job', Geoff informed Simon, as they ate their evening tea.'

Simon was waiting for the football results, and not really listening to Geoff's chatter.

'What do you recon they will get then?' he asked, more out of politeness than interest.

'It was the biggest job since the great train robbery you know', Geoff informed him. 'Too early to say what the sentence will be, but no one got hurt, so they could not get done for G.B.H'.

They always went out on Friday night. Only along the road to the Fisherman's Rest where they had a fish and chip supper and a couple of pints.

'I thought we would take a run over to see Pete on Wednesday, you know, Pete the egg man from Margate. I am thinking of getting a scooter like he has', Geoff suggested.

'Sounds good, and a good idea to ask Pete, he's had a scooter for years. Goes all over the place with it'.

They did not stay late. It was getting busy with tourists now, and there was more comfort sitting at home in their own place. So, once they had finished their meal, and just the two pints, they were back home again.

'Be nice to have a run out on Wednesday, no arrivals that day, so no need to rush back', Simon informed Geoff. But he was talking to himself as Geoff had dozed off in the armchair.

Time for Simon to make their bedtime drink, and then call it a day. Three couples leaving in the morning, and two arriving in the afternoon. Busy day tomorrow.

****

Pete the 'egg man' was everyone's vision of Father Christmas. His rotund figure and his long white beard always caused quite a stir amongst the young, and not so young, in December.

But truth be known Pete is as much into receiving as giving, and this had been his main source of income for many years. That and his disability pension, for his mobility is limited, and he uses an electric scooter when outside his home.

Home, officially, is a well-kept bungalow in Margate. But Pete enjoys travelling. Once Christmas is over, and the fun of seeing the faces of small children mesmerized with a mixture of joy and disbelief, Pete heads off for the balmy weather in Malta. There he meets with a group of friends at the Canifor Hotel, and being only a short trip to Sicily, takes the opportunity to meet business contacts as well.

At the end of March, Pete goes back home to check his post and pay any outstanding bills, and until this past two years, by mid-April would be off travelling again. And usually to Rhodes.

Pete had been going to Rhodes Island for more than twenty-five years. Like many returning tourists, he had stumbled across this Greek island when looking for an inexpensive teletext holiday. And for his side-line as a 'fence' and sometimes a financial 'go between' to the rich and famous, it proved a great asset. Not only were many of the residents Italian, so one more made no difference if they called to see him, but almost everyone spoke English. What more could you want on a Greek island? Also, there were many English tourists, who took small parcels for him, and posted them on when back in the U.K. In Kent, Malta, and Rhodes, he was known to everyone as 'Pete the egg man'.

Pete has an amazing artistic skill, decorating eggs in a style made famous by Faberge. Sometimes duck eggs and often Ostrich eggs when available. The only difference between the work of Faberge and Pete was that Pete occasionally put his precious gems on the inside. When at home, he has a small workshop in the Birchington Craft Village, and at least three days a week he goes there to indulge his hobby, making gifts to order for weddings and birthdays, and, naturally, a few extra for himself.

How long had he known Geoff? So long ago that he had forgotten. For all that they were vaguely aware of being in the same line of business, and these days attending the same funerals, they never discussed this side of their life.

The note Pete had sent to Geoff was neat and to the point.

Fancy a pint, usual place, could be a busy summer.

It seemed strange that ordinary 'snail mail' was the safest way to contact someone these days.

It was when Simon had gone to the counter to order their lunch of steak and kidney pie, that Pete asked Geoff if he was still working.

'Just a little bit here and there, no point in getting your fingers burnt at my time of life'.

'That is what I hoped you would say. I have a small parcel to pick up in Greece. Small but heavy, if you understand me, and the payoff will set you up for life'.

'Or get me life' Geoff joked. Pete was not amused.

'Your choice, in or out', he asked.

'As I said, never been to Greece, and time I had a holiday.

I will tell Simon just about a holiday, nothing else, and he will be up for it. I would not go without him, could not manage on my own these days'.

'No problem, So two tickets. Will look good with both of you and a wheelchair, could not be better'.

Simon arrived back at the table. He would not have another pint, not worth getting your license marked up. They agreed another pint would spoil their lunch and had a coffee and walnut cake to round off their meal.

When Simon went to the bar to pay, Pete resumed the conversation.

'Might not be for a while yet. Just see how things go. If you change your mind, let me know. And if I have doubts about it, I will shout loud and clear. Would do it myself but I cannot manage the steps and uneven pavements in Greece now'. Geoff was wondering what the connection was, but Simon was back, so they changed the subject quickly.

'I tell you the thing you need around here is that new bike gadget. It clips onto the wheelchair and has an engine like a small moped. But, if you decide on the same make of scooter as I have, contact Keith as he has the franchise for these machines. Mention my name and you might get a good deal'.

Simon was pleased Geoff had a friend. Give him something to think about and cheer him up. He was becoming a bit of a dreary old sod. Must be the arthritis, Simon concluded.

They took a steady drive back, mostly along the coast, and watched the sea turn red in the light of the setting sun. Geoff was pleased to have something to think about other than buying a disability scooter. Something of a gut feeling told him it could be connected to that diamond heist. The main haul had not yet been found. Stupid to speculate at this stage.

Geoff was right, there was a connection. But it was some weeks later before he heard from Pete again.

I will call over to you on Friday, no problem getting a lift, meet at the bar for lunch? The note had said.

Now Simon and Geoff were sitting on the bench outside the Fisherman's Rest, waiting in the pleasant summer sun. Pete arrived on time, and Simon got up to help him from the cab of the delivery truck. The driver, a neighbour of Pete's, said he would be back in about an hour and a half. He would stop and have a pint with them before taking Pete home to Margate.

It was starting to rain, so they went inside and once seated, and Simon had gone to the bar to order their lunch, Pete gave Geoff an envelope. 'The tickets are inside. You go to Rhodes first, to pick up some special buttons. All details are written down. You have to give the guy a card to collect them. Then over to an island called Symi. It depends which side of the harbour the boat docks how near the leather shop you are when you get off the ferry. But it is a small harbour, with shops and cafes. Anyone will know Takis leather shop. You can take your time, have a coffee nearby, wait until the shop is empty. Takis always stands outside when there are no customers inside. He is expecting you and has 'country and western' style leather waistcoats made for both you and Simon. All pre- paid, just hand him this business card. I suggest you wear them coming through the customs. Make a statement if you follow my meaning. He will only give the gear to the man with a card, so don't leave home without it', Pete laughed.

Fortunately for Geoff and Pete, Simon had met a friend at the bar and stayed chatting to him. He returned when their lunch was served. Fish and chips and mushy peas. What more could a man want?

A few weeks later Geoff spoke about going to Greece.

There were two bookings for the guest house on the date Geoff was suggesting for the holiday. Both couples had been coming for years. The people knew each other and were staying for the usual two weeks.

'Offer them half price, and tell them to look after themselves', Geoff suggested to Simon.

'O.K, I'll leave the keys next door, no problem'. And in that way, it was sorted.

He told the girls. 'So where are you going dad', they asked. 'Greece', he replied. 'Yes, but where in Greece?' Shelly insisted. 'How should I know'. It suddenly dawned on him that he had not a clue, but if Geoff had the tickets, he did not really care. 'When your uncle Geoff organizes, I don't ask questions. You should know that by now'.

Mind you it was a long time since Geoff had organized anything. Where they were going and why, suddenly had Simon's full attention. Well, it did until the television was on and Spurs were playing Man U., then it went straight out of his head as quickly as it had come in just half an hour ago.

****

Carol Webb had enjoyed her week in Lindos with the craft group better than any holiday she had ever had. Well, apart from their honeymoon years ago, but a honeymoon is different, she reasoned to herself. The only thing was the holiday on Rhodes unsettled her for quite a while once she came back. She decided that she needed to make some changes to her life, and one of those changes was to look for a new job. It was several weeks before she saw something that interested her, and it was within Social Services and Housing. Carol knew she could find out more about it through the grape vine of her Home Care friends.

The council needed a new manager for the Sheltered Housing flats at the other end of Chiswick high street. She had been in the building many times before, when visiting Home Care clients. Carol was still not sure she was doing the right thing, but the Sheltered Housing post sounded more sociable than her present job, though she had no illusions that it would be a piece of cake. But her friends were very encouraging.

'It would make our job much easier having someone on our side, you know what a miserable witch that Thelma was. You did not get the offer of a coffee or chat, even if you have ten minutes to spare, or the nurse is in with one of the clients. Go for it girl', Jean had told her.

Anyway, the interview went well, and she already had her police clearance, so no delay if she was offered the job. And the hours were good, eight till two five days a week, no shifts or evening work. Call centres and mobile phones had certainly changed the job since she had last enquired about being a 'Warden', as they called it in those days.

'Don't start going on about it till they offer it to you', Richie had suggested to her yesterday. 'You get really keen on something, and start agonizing on how you will cope, what the people will be like, and it might be for nothing. Though if they find anyone better than you, I would be most surprised', he added hastily just in case she misunderstood his comments. He knew what she was like but could never understand why she had this lack of confidence.

D.I. Richard Webb had been married to Carol for almost twenty years. They might have liked a couple of kids, but none came their way and eventually they quietly accepted that was how it would be, just the two of them. It helped that they both had quite different but demanding jobs, although Carol found it lonely in the evenings when he was on a late shift.

For Richie, he never seemed to notice. He was a blokes' bloke. Enjoying fishing holidays with his mates, never thinking to ask Carol where she would like to go, or if she could get the same week off work. But on returning from a craft holiday on a Greek island, he thought how great she looked. Perhaps it was time he thought of sitting on a Greek beach himself. He was getting too old to spend a week up to his thighs in cold muddy water and, though he hated to admit it, too old to then spend the night in a pub, downing pints of draft Guinness.

This morning there was a briefing at eleven o'clock. He guessed it would be about the stabbing in the tube station last night. Grabbing a coffee from the machine, he wandered in, surprised to see so many 'top brass'. He was wrong, it was not concerning the stabbing; they were back discussing the diamond heist again.

'We now have it on good authority that one of our suspects high tailed it to Greece. To an island near Turkey called Symi. No airport there, so you must get a flight to Athens or Rhodes and a boat. Does anyone know the area I am talking about?' he asked.

'I had two weeks on Kos last year', John Harris offered. There was a ripple of amusement.

'I can go one better', Richie told them. 'My wife was on Rhodes a few weeks ago, on a craft holiday. Nice place she said'.

'Now we are getting somewhere. I presume she would like to go again?'

'I presume she would Sir', Richie replied.

Now the meeting moved on to the stabbing incident and by the time they were updated on that it was lunch time.

'Well, sod me', John remarked once they were safely out of earshot. 'Who's a jammy bastard then?'

'Some you win', Richie replied, with a shrug of his shoulders.

But to be honest he was not sure that he wanted to be that close to the modern equivalent of the 'Diamond Geezers'. His father had told him many tales about that tough gang with the Robin Hood reputation, based in East London after the war.

Later that afternoon he was summoned to the small upstairs office. Once introductions were made, the door was closed, and they sat down.

'We had a tip off, now known to the public thanks to the Daily Mail, about the guy reported to be on Symi island, a small place near Rhodes. Two of our men are there but we need back up in case the suspect returns to Rhodes. Or, if he stays on Symi, as it is only a small place, we need to change the tag every now and again. If he goes off to Athens, then you can sit in the sun until he returns. But an ordinary tourist couple would be less obvious than a couple of 'flat foots' mooching around. You speak a bit of Italian they tell me?'

'From my grandparents Sir, so probably a bit rusty', Richie replied, wondering what Italian had to do with Greece.

'The brief is that you are attending a conference about the refugee situation. Not that the Med is our problem yet, but it looks good to be represented. And there genuinely is a series of meetings. Just turn up to one or two will do, as it is only a courtesy invite. Otherwise do the tourist bit and mingle in the bars once we know where the guy is'.

'I am sure I can manage that Sir, not a problem'. His superior officers greeted the comment in the way it was meant, and as Richie had presumed, the meeting was over. He was just going through the office door when he remembered about Carol.

'Slight problem Sir. My wife has just applied for a new job. If she gets offered it they may want her to start straight away, and if she does not she has no holiday time left till September'.

'Nothing to worry about, we can organize that, if need be, but stick to the story please, even with your wife'.

'No problem. Sir, when do we pack?'

Carol got the job with the sheltered housing, but to her surprise they did not want her to start till next month. She worked out her notice and found it hard to believe she was on her way to Rhodes again. And with Richie? And all paid for? And they would be staying at Koki apartments again? What a strange turn of events!

Early next morning she went down Chiswick high street, and into Marks and Sparks. First, she treated herself to a new swimming costume and then took the escalator upstairs, to the café for a coffee. She chose a scone, complete with jam and cream. After all she was officially on holiday.

****

PART 5

Ruth had never kept it a secret! After all, in her experience it was a common place item in most households. How the word spread around Lindos that she had one, she could only guess. And before long she was being asked to do small projects on her sewing machine on a regular basis.

Well, the projects started off quite small, like turning a hem on the trousers Tina had cut to make into shorts, and to recover the cushions on Christian's chair he used in the garden.

Then John Nightingale rang, apologizing for having asked Tanya to pass on Ruth's number.

'The thing is', he started with some hesitation, 'The thing is I run a water sports concession down on the beach in Kiotari. The seat covers on my speed boat are beginning to look a bit shabby, and please would you make me some new ones? I have already bought some material that I think will do for the job, and I was told you have a sewing machine'.

Ruth hesitated at first. She explained that she had a sewing machine but was not an upholsterer.

'Oh, don't worry about that', he told her. 'They are only foam cushions, with a bit of spare to cover the engine'.

Ruth said that she would need to see what she was undertaking before agreeing to help. So, it was arranged for John to call around to the spiti that evening to show Ruth the heavy quality denim he had bought. She assured him it would work well on her machine, and they set the day, early the next week for John to take Ruth down to Kiotari where the boat was parked, (or should it be moored?) In the courtyard, over a scotch and ice, they chatted about John's childhood, spent on various RAF bases, both in England and in Germany.

'You never know what might come in handy later in life', he explained. 'When I wanted to teach skiing in Austria, my basic German landed me the job', he told Ruth. He had already pointed out that he could not bring all the cushions to Lindos, as they would be wet at the end of the day, and he would need them next morning.

Anyway, Ruth had never been to Kiotari, and Thursday she was up early, ready to enjoy her day out.

It was lovely to be driving off in the morning, when the air was fresh and the sun sending a silver stream of light across the sea. But to her surprise they headed inland.

'It is quicker this way than going along the coast', John explained. 'And I need to pick up petrol for the boat'.

When, after only a short drive they stopped at a garage, Ruth was surprised to see John load two big canisters into the back of his small car. Was this petrol? Was it safe? She laughed at herself. After all this is Greece and no doubt, he had been doing thing in the same way for a long time, and without problems. Though to be honest she did not relax again until the canisters were unloaded onto the beach at Kiotari.

The scenery on the way down had switched with every twist and turn of the road. One minute a beautiful sea view, and the next a barren mountain side. There were the occasional large hotels and some small villages. And when they left the main road to go down to the sea, she saw a long beach, with sunbeds topped by umbrellas.

Ruth was introduced to other people working with the water sports. Taking the coffee offered, she looked around, trying to take everything in.

She presumed the boat in question was anchored a few yards into the water. But from her vantage point she could not see any seating area. A few minutes later she saw John returned with a cushion.

'I should have asked for them to be left in the drying shed this morning, but it never entered my head', he told her honestly.

'Not a problem, if, as you say, they are all the same size'.

'Well, that is the problem, I think two are different'.

'Shall I just measure this and make one this evening and you can try it out tomorrow. At least it will be a start'.

Ruth took her tape measure and writing pad from her bag.

One of the first trips out for John that morning was towing a large plastic sofa with six teenagers sitting on it. Naturally they were all given lifejackets, and he invited Ruth to come onto the boat, just to see what they got up to. She also had a lifejacket, as did John, and removing her sandals, expected to wade into the cool sea. But he brought the boat around to a small wooden jetty so that she could easily clamber aboard.

She was so pleased she was in the boat rather than on the plastic float. John twisted and turned the speed boat to the delight of the passengers trailing behind, as one would expect from a group of young people. John spoke to Ruth without taking his eyes off his charges, and when one lad started to drag his feet over the edge, he immediately stopped the boat and made him sit back safely.

For Ruth, the thrill was being able to look back along the coastline. There were white painted hotels rising high above the cliffs, and beyond them the bare mountains. The contrast was breath-taking. And every so often, little homes, dwarfed by the hotels, were dotted along the hillsides.

Back on the beach Ruth left John to his next customers, and as arranged, she walked back up to the main road. She had checked out the buses and sat and had a coffee and croissant whilst she waited. And if she had not got a sewing machine, she doubted she would have spent a morning all at sea with the water sports in Kiotari.

****

On Tuesday they were back with Stathis. 'We are having a social hour after the Friday dance class next week. Just a light buffet, and a glass of wine'. Later he spoke to Bertie about it and invited them to stay over at his apartment in Canada Street.

'I have a twin bed spare room, also a bed-settee in the lounge, so I will leave it up to you as to how you designate the accommodation, but you are very welcome', he assured them.

They enjoyed the social hour, particularly having time to chat to Andonis and Zenia, and with Eleni from Asklipios. It was over too quick, but they did not have to rush to catch a bus as they had accepted Stathis' invitation at stay overnight.

Once at the lovely apartment, they declined the offer of a nightcap, and fell into the comfortable beds with exhaustion.

The next morning, they were up and showered early, but Stathis had beaten them to it, and the smell of percolating coffee filled the kitchen-diner.

They declined anything more than toast and marmalade, and Bertie enjoyed a strong black coffee. Ruth was pleased to be offered a Nescafe alternative.

Once they were all seated around the breakfast table, Ruth asked Stathis which part of Greece he came from.

'Well, thereby hangs a tale, as, although I am Greek, we are actually from Turkey'.

'At one time, around the beginning of the last century, there were many Greeks living around the area of Constantinople, or should I say Istanbul. There were also many Turkish Muslim families in these island areas of Greece'.

'Anyway, there was talk of an exchange of population, rather like happened in India many years later. For the ordinary people it was a catastrophe waiting to happen. In fact, it was my maternal great grandfather's Turkish barber who warned him to leave. I do not know what prompted my father's father, but I expect it was Turkish friends and associates. Both sides of my family were well established, owning residential property and business premises. They came from the village of Kerasia, in an area called Thrace. It is the only European part of modern Turkey. As I explained it is not far from Istanbul. And they travelled from there to Boston'.

Stathis gazed out across the sea, not to the Turkey on the skyline, but to an immigrant childhood in America. 'I have many fond memories of my grandparents.

He continued. 'I was born in Boston as was my mother, Olympia.

My maternal grandparents had been amongst the thousands of Greeks pre-empting being expelled from turkey in 1922. Olympia's parents came from Constantinople, where Orthodox Christians living in Turkey were exchanged for Muslims living in Greece'.

Coffee cups were refilled.

'It seems strange now to think that a British diplomat was involved in the process, though it seems there was no diplomacy only a threat from the Turks to massacre the people of Greek origin. For the ordinary families, it was just as hard for the Greek Muslims. They also left their homes, to find land in a country where they could not speak the language. There were few homes with amenities such as they had in Greece. The threat was initially two weeks to leave, but no Greek boats were allowed into the Turkish harbour to transport them. Then the date was extended by another two weeks, and that was considered a major concession.

Ruth could not but help comparing it with her own family's migration from Ireland to England when she was a child. There was no comparison really, but for a child, the uprooting from everything familiar, was a devastating experience.

And the sad thing is, it is still going on today, she thought.

They chatted on about other things, where they had first learnt to dance, how it was both exciting and terrifying going into a dance hall, even the one run by the local church.

Then Stathis said he would walk with them, to show them a short cut from Canada Street into the New Town.

'Shall I see you again on Tuesday?', Stathis asked.

'Certainly, the dance classes have become the highlights of our week', Bertie assured him, and on that note, they parted company, Ruth and Bertie easily found the bus station, and were soon on their way back to Lindos.

'What fascinates me about living on Rhodes', Bertie informed Ruth, 'You never know how the week, will turn out'.

How true, she thought.

****

The farmhouse in Asklipious had been rented out for the summer. The lady was American. She had been to Lindos before, but her friends had not.

The friends travelling to Rhodes were from quite different backgrounds. Shirley lived in Seattle, not far from where Henrietta had her bungalow. But Deana was from London, her late husband a former R.A.F. officer. Henrietta had met Deana more than thirty years ago, and if passing through London, was always made welcome at her Kensington apartment. But if London was for shopping, then Rhodes was for sun and sandy beaches. A relaxing 'girlie' holiday.

'We plan to do some sightseeing during the vacation but for the first week all we want to do is to relax by the pool'.

There was no pool. Heather did not manage the bookings so should she inform them herself or tell Trish? She decided on the latter and let them sort it out between them.

'Unusual really as Americans are mostly well organized and would have double checked', she told Tracy later when they met outside the Flovaris supermarket. How was Heather to know that Henrietta was quite the least organized person on either continent?

Bertie was pleased with the deal he had secured for Henrietta and her friends. Admittedly there was no pool but there was quite a nice hot tub around the back. It was some time since he had been down there, certainly not since Tim and Trish had gone back to England. They had kindly suggested he might like to go and stay for a week before the guests arrived and this he decided to do. Not for a week, but he rather fancied a few days of seclusion. He did not think to mention this to Ruth, particularly as she had company anyway, and Bertie had disappeared from Lindos as easily as he had appeared just a few weeks earlier.

He had Heather's phone number and would stop by at the caravan for the keys. They had met briefly before when she was on the craft course the previous year. The group had taken a minibus to Rhodes Old Town, and he had joined the trip, sitting next to Heather at dinner that night in Romeo's. Then their paths crossed again, at Nefeli restaurant, on the last night of this year's craft group.

He decided to take a leisurely drive down in the hire car he had booked for Henrietta and her friends. And having the whole day at his disposal he stopped at Coralli, just outside Pefcos, for a swim before lunch.

He did not like swimming in pools as a rule but the infinity pool at Coralli was the exception. Spacious and with nothing but sea and sky it was refreshing with the bonus of coffee or ice cream on hand at the poolside, or something stronger if you wished. And the beach and the sea were only at the bottom of the steps. Most pool side sun beds were empty during the day as many of the residents were out exploring nearby Lindos or other parts of the island.

The greeting from Tsambica was as warm as ever. This was a truly family run restaurant, as her mother was often on hand, as were her husband and son. He sat on the comfy sofas with his coffee and home- made pastry.

'This all looks very festive', he remarked admiring the decorations hanging from the roof beams and the long tables with white covered chairs, each sporting a blue silk bow.

'We have a wedding later this evening and had one yesterday, so we are extra busy this week'.

Bertie had to admit he could not think of a more perfect setting. It was obviously a non-Greek couple as there was no way Tsambica could host the four hundred guests that attended local nuptials. He thought it would be a lovely venue to bring Ruth to, somewhere different that he was sure she would not have visited before. He was aware of intruding into her memories of Max and wished to leave the places the couple had frequented last year as just that; memories. He left the lounge area and walked the few yards to the almost empty pool and an inviting wooden sun bed. This is the life he thought, but wished Ruth was with him to share the day.

It was late afternoon when he left Coralli, having enjoyed a relaxing swim, a lovely lunch, and a glass of wine. He had one more call to make, to see his friend Panagiotis at the folk museum, then he would be on his way south.

Only a few hundred yards further on he pulled into the spacious car park. Stepping out of the car he stopped for a moment to admire the building. The signs were up and looked exceedingly good. Everything was neat and well ordered, and the apricot trees were laden with fruit. Panagiotis sat at a small table near the open door. He strode out to greet his English friend.

'Well, my old friend, this looks very impressive', Bertie told him. Panagiotis smiled and looked up to admire the façade of the building himself.

'It was a long time coming but I am pleased with the results, come inside and look around'. He waived Bertie's offer to pay the three-euro entry fee. 'How will you survive if you do not allow people to pay', Bertie asked, but got a look of distain from Panagiotis, which clearly said he would be offended if it was mentioned again.

They wandered around looking at the old village pictures and the ancient agricultural machinery and chatting about the ten-year struggle to make the museum a reality. Panagiotis had hawked his history books around the restaurants of Lindos and Lardos each summer until he had raised the money for his project. Bertie spotted some pottery for sale and chose a plate for Henrietta as a welcome gift. Well pleased with his visit he wished his friend a good summer, with lots of visitors, and drove on down to Asklipios.

****

When Bertie knocked on the door of the caravan Heather invited him in for coffee. He was surprised at the space once inside, though naturally he had to bend quite low to get in the door. But that was often the case for ordinary bricks and mortar houses, and he was quite used to it. He looked around the cosy living room with its dining table at one end, and the bench seating, comfortable yet practical.

'We are so lucky to be in this amazing space', Heather told him. 'Sometimes it can get a bit quiet in the evenings, once Lucy is in bed, but I have the internet connection, and do face book with my sisters and friends. And Skype mum and dad every Saturday evening. I still do a school run for two couples who are working. Not from this village as there is a good school here but ex pats who live this side of Lindos. It pays for petrol and insurance on the car. Dad came out to visit a few weeks ago, and will be back again later this year, he really enjoyed it. So, all is good'. With that he thanked Heather for the coffee, took the keys and went off towards the house.

Heather quite enjoyed being there on her own, but that would change now the Americans were on their way, she was sure.

Bertie found the house larger than he remembered. The view over the fields to the sea was stunning. The building was horseshoe shaped, with an open courtyard in the centre. It was an ingenious design in that you could choose to sit in the sun or the shade at any time of day, and still have a view of the sea. The rocky mound at the back protected it from the wind on the land side. Once inside he could see how the original and traditional oblong building had been extended to the shape it now was. Tim and Trish had stored their personal stuff in one area leaving the rest of the house available to sublet.

Bertie was delighted with what he saw, and so immaculate; there was nothing he needed to do but sit and relax for a few days, or for as long as he wished, as Henrietta had invited him to join them at the house during their stay. And after the first night's sleep, only broken in the morning by a goat on the roof, he was totally hooked.

He was looking forward to seeing Henrietta again, and had met Shirley often during the three years he had spent in the States. He thought they would enjoy their stay in Asklipios.   And why not stay on for that first few days, just until they got their bearings. He could suggest places they should visit. Yes, why not? Shame about the pool.

****

And it was just over a week later that Ruth returned to Asklipios. Her friend Holly Schofield was back on Rhodes for a holiday, and as she had a rental car, suggested the day out.

They did not see anywhere they fancied as a coffee stop until they were in the village. Once Holly had found a parking space, they headed for the bakery. It was rather hot outside, so they chose a seat by the window. In that way they could see village comings and goings but take advantage of the aircon. Comfortably settled with their latte and vanilla slice, they fell into the people watching they both enjoyed.

'When I first came here, I assumed anyone wearing the long, traditional black garments must be in their eighties, but I understand some women go into mourning for a relative when quite young and never go back to colourful attire', Ruth said, when a lady passed by dressed in black from head to toe.

'They do not get the chance, as mourning lasts for three years', Holly told her. 'By the time three years are up, once you are a certain age, another relation has passed away, and so it goes'.

It was then that Ruth noticed a tall man with an unusual gait and immediately knew it was Bertie. She was just about to say something when she realised that the lady he was walking towards was the American, Henrietta. There were other women with them, one small and dark haired, and the other a tall, good looking blonde. Bertie took her hand as they crossed the road. They were laughing and chatting noisily.

Holly turned to see what or who had grabbed Ruth's attention.

'Do you know those people? she asked. 'Shall we call and invite them to join us?' but Holly could see from Ruth's face that it was not really on the agenda. She bit her tongue, though curious to know the connection.

'Anyway, do you fancy another coffee? We could stay here for lunch if you like?' she added, thinking that it would give time for the other people to leave, if that was what Ruth wanted.

Ruth shook her head.' No, thank you, if it is still alright with you, I would rather stick to our plan and go to Pefkos. This is nice, but I prefer to sit by the sea, and there is shaded outside space at Coralli', Ruth replied.

They settled the bill and left the café. They wandered around the small village, getting caught up in the avalanche of little ones leaving the school. They both looked with saddened eyes as granddads put five- year- old children onto their mopeds and went off down the road, neither adult nor child wearing a crash helmet. No doubt they loved their grandchildren dearly yet could not see how they risked the youngsters' lives. It was the same all over the island, with rare exceptions, but not something Ruth ever got accustomed to.

It did not take long to locate the church and the little museum. They wandered leisurely around both before returning to the car. It was only a twenty-minute drive, this time along the main highway, before they reached their destination.

Tsambika greeted them in her usual friendly way. They were shown out to a paved area next to the pool. Each space had its own secluded, and rather intimate, shaded seating area. There was a cool breeze from the sea below, so even in the late afternoon it was not uncomfortably hot. Soon they were seated and looking at the menus. They decided to share a Greek salad and lamb chops. To drink they chose a glass of white wine.

'I was being rather silly not introducing you to Bertie', Ruth began. Holly raised her hand. 'You owe me no explanation, not a problem', she said hastily.

'It is just I thought he was in Rhodes and I did not realise that Henrietta was over from the States. I have not seen her since Max died and I did not want to sit though very kindly meant condolences, not today'.

'I understand, and I do agree with you, it is difficult when suddenly confronted with that situation. A wise move I would say. If she is on

Rhodes for long, then no doubt there will be other occasions. It is only a small island'.

And in this way the subject was glossed over, and they sipped their wine, looking out beyond the infinity pool to the sea.

If Holly thought that there was more to Ruth's reaction than the explanation given, she kept such thoughts to herself. And Ruth had no idea why she should object to Bertie being in Asklipios or anywhere else for that matter and with anyone he please to choose as a companion. It really was none of her concern. So why was she concerned, she asked herself as she munched on her salad.

****

NIGEL HAD BEEN in Prasonissi for seven weeks.

He had taken his time, walking around chatting to people, both young and old, telling them about the evening campfire sessions he planned to start on the following Sunday.

At first these got off to a slow start, but there was a regular core of people. Some had guitars and played and sang, contributing to the atmosphere. There were ready and willing translators for his brief talks. One older Austrian couple started bringing feta and spinach pies, cut into small bites and passed around. Others followed their example and soon Nigel had to ask people to take some food away with them at the end of the evening to save it being wasted.

Gradually people came to look for him in the early evening, and often in broken English would tell him of their concerns, their nomadic lifestyle, lack of contact with their family, a multitude of different worries.

He decided to have a special quiet hour on Friday evenings. He distributed pencils and paper bought from the local gift shop and those who wished wrote down their prayers. As the campfire smouldered, they were invited to place their petitions into the fire. The heart felt notes, scribbled onto pieces of torn notepad would ascend with the smoke. Guitars played softly, and many strong men and hippy girls shed tears in the dark. At the end of the quiet hour, Nigel softly sang one of his favourite hymns.

The following morning, a young couple came to chat.

'That hymn you sang last night, 'What a friend we have in Jesus', I have never heard anything like it. Do you think I can get the words from somewhere?

'I will get them printed out for you. But like everything else these days, it is on You Tube. Are you from Ireland? Nigel asked them. They told him they were from Island Bridge, on the edge of Dublin.

'The writer of that hymn was born in Dublin, but after a tragedy in his life he moved to Ontario in Canada, His name was Joseph Scrivin.'

'Wow, what a strange coincidence. I mean us being from Dub and you from Canada'. The young people thanked Nigel for his help and said they would be at the campfire Sunday night.

Nigel went into the Lighthouse restaurant looking for Asimeni. The hinge had come loose on the back door and she had asked him earlier if he would fix it, as her dad had gone up to Rhodes town for the day. It was the least he could do, and like Joseph Scrivin, enjoyed using his skills to help people.

Why he had travelled so far that summer he did not really know, but it had been many years since he had been to Greece, and he needed a holiday, and …….

So, although some weeks away, come the end of September he planned to have a few lazy days in Asklipios, making sure there was nothing that he needed to do for Heather at the caravan. And with his flights already booked, he would be off to Canada and home again. Everything was falling into place, how blessed he had been.

****

BERTIE HAD RETURNED to England. 'It is only for a week. Just legal stuff to sort out', he had told Ruth.

At least he had told her, not like when she thought he was in Rhodes and then she saw him in Asklipios with Henrietta and her friends. She had never raised that point, and whilst it kept niggling away, she had decided that, if she was going to continue her affair with Bertie, she must accept him as he was. And she had thought about their 'affair', quite a lot.

In many ways, she was betraying principles she had held dear all her life. But her inner self argued, times had changed. And was she being old fashioned, and making a fuss about nothing? Certainly, there were no children to consider and he was free, not someone else's husband. And she had no other commitments or obligations to anyone except herself. And recent conversations with people she had met in and around Lindos made her wonder if she was the only person who considered such things.

It was when having coffee with Peggy on the rooftop of Delight that the subject first arose.

'Do you and Bertie have any plans to make things legal, or are you going to jog along like the rest of us do these days?' Ruth nearly choked on her latte. She did not think that anyone in Lindos would know of her relationship.

'Oh sorry, have I said the wrong thing?' Peggy asked. 'No, no, it just came as a shock to think people knew about Bertie', Ruth said, reaching for her handkerchief. Peggy laughed. 'Do you know even God himself does not know what happens in Lindos better than the people here, particularly the expats. You should know by now that you cannot go in one door or out of another without being observed by someone'.

'But you are not in Lindos. You live in Kalathos', Ruth reminded her.

Peggy was quiet for a moment. Ruth did not know what to say. It was the first time she had known Peggy to be other than her bright and cheerful self. 'Don't let me be a wet blanket, I am sure you and Bertie will work things out in a sensible way'.

They finished their coffee and parted company. It had certainly given Ruth a lot to think about. She had just accepted that anyone they knew presumed she and Bertie were just old friends who occasionally enjoyed a meal out together. However, in the past few weeks it was not the first conversation where marital status had been the subject.

'We're not married you know', Cath confided. Ruth smiled and continued to add butter and marmalade to her croissant, not sure why a 'more than middle aged' lady, of obvious impeccable middle England taste, had decided to offer such information to herself, a stranger.

Well, Ruth considered herself to be a stranger to this nice lady she had now met twice at Giorgos Two.

They had shared the same table for a morning coffee, Ruth, Cath and Bernard, Cath's husband or as it turned out, not her husband!

'We met here two years ago, just having a coffee', Cath explained whilst Bernard read the sports pages of yesterday's Mail. 'There were some children playing on the sand, and the youngest one fell over into the sea and started to howl like a banshee', she continued. 'We both laughed, and I asked Bernard if he had grandchildren. That started us chatting about family and being on your own, and by then it was lunch time. The rest is what they call history', she laughed.

'We sold our houses, gave most of the proceeds to the children and bought a spacious mobile home in Hurley, near the Thames. Beautiful place, we have our own small garden area and private patio'. Bernard looked up and smiled, Ruth guessed he had not missed a word of the conversation.

'How lovely for you both', Ruth said, and was pleased for this happy elderly couple, relaxing in the sun.

If that had been the only occasion such a conversation had taken place, apart from her chat the previous week with Peggy, she would have thought no more about it.

A few days later she was on the bus going up to Rhodes town, when a grey-haired lady sat next to her, and started to chat.

'Where are you staying love', she said with a northern accent.

'In Lindos', Ruth truthfully replied.

'How long are you staying for, one week or two?'

'Well actually I live here, in Lindos', and pre-empting the next question added, 'I came on holiday last year and never really went back'.

'Well good for you, I think I would if I was on my own', the lady Ruth soon knew as Irene had replied. 'I still could if I wanted to as we're not married you know'. She nodded her head to a tall gentleman in brown corduroy sitting in the seat across the aisle. 'He won't risk it, moving abroad. 'There is for and against', Ruth replied, though she could not think of any reason against living on Rhodes, but people did not want to be told they only had to make the decision and the rest was quite easy if you did not want to buy property.

They chatted on, well Irene did, about the rising cost of living and that the government had taken money away from the winter fuel allowance but eventually Irene was asking Ruth the best places to visit whilst in Rhodes town. Ruth had explained about the old town and how to get there, and that it was also a nice walk along Mandraki harbour if they had time before catching the bus back to Lindos later in the day.

'Enjoy your holiday', Ruth told her as they parted company.

The next people she met in Rhodes town that day were also not married. Ruth had met Andrea and David Hubble the first week she was on Rhodes. She sat near them one afternoon in Georgios bar. Andrea and David were brother and sister. Both living independently, they planned their first holiday to Lindos. They enjoyed it so much they had been regular visitors for several years. They all laughed at bumping into each other in town and agreed to have coffee in Georgios later that week.

Sitting alone, eating an ice cream along Mandraki harbour, try as she could, Ruth found it hard to no think about her relationship with Bertie. And Irene on the bus was not young but a mature adult, throwing convention to the wind.

She knew her brother Francis would be delighted for her to have Bertie in her life. In many ways that was all the approval she needed. How Francis would have enjoyed Rhodes. For Francis that special place would have been anywhere where he would have been accepted for who he was.

Her thoughts went back to the nine years they had shared their lives, never had she volunteered the information that she and Francis were brother and sister and not, as everyone seemed to assume, a couple. But of course, they had other far more important reasons for keeping their own counsel. Such assumptions suited their way of life for those years they spent in

Canterbury, and it was no one's concern but their own.

And now here she was sharing a marital bed with Bertie. But that was Bertie, and for some strange reason Ruth felt comfortable in his arms without any formality or even any agreement to move into a more formal relationship. It was not on the agenda. Ruth assumed that sooner or later he would be off on another plane, and she smiled at the pun. For Bertie was often 'off on another plane'.

'Oh dear, like everything in life, it will be 'a matter of conscience', she concluded, and for some strange reason, which she decided not to sit and ponder a moment longer, her conscience seemed remarkably clear.

So why did she not tell Father Paul when she spoke to him on the phone yesterday? He had asked about Bertie, and she had told him that, yes, he was in Rhodes, and yes, he was a good friend, and they ate out together a couple of times a week. 'Do you now', was his response to that. Maybe she could not hide much from him, after all they had been friends for longer than either of them cared to remember.

PART 6

FOR CAROL THERE WAS no comparison between her experience at Heathrow this time and her anxious wait for the flight to Rhodes just a few weeks ago.

Richie had the tickets, so she did not need to get stressed about which desk to go to. Carol just walked hand in hand with her husband and smiled. Once the formalities were over, they stopped at a bar where he ordered a large Scotch for himself and a Bacardi and coke for her.

'Get this down. It will do you good'. He watched Carol taste her drink before he took a sip of his own.

'To be honest I had forgotten you do not like flying. Sorry about that, you should have said,' Carol smiled back. 'Not a problem when I am with you. It was a bit of a minefield when on my own. Though I think I am better since the last trip. Or maybe it is just having the company'.

It did not really matter which, as everything felt different this time. She smiled at her husband, but half of her smile was recalling the company she had enjoyed on the last flight. Her 'Rossano Brassi' look alike, who managed to distract her from thinking about the turbulence.

She was so pleased to meet up with him again during a day trip on the Magelanos. That evening, invited to his hotel in Kolymbia, she enjoyed supper with Felice and his lovely wife and children.

But that was history and she still found it hard to believe she was once again in the airport, waiting for a flight to Rhodes. And she knew she did not even have to look on the board to choose the gate, let alone find her way to it.

They spent some time sitting comfortably at the bar, sipping their drinks, and reading the Daily Mail, Carol scanning the women's page and glancing at the star sign predictions and Richie immersed in the sports pages.

Both were pleased that the Aegean flight was on time. The flight was uneventful, and after another drink they dosed off.

In no time at all they were landing. The evening air hit them with an unexpected rush of warmth.

As they made their way across the tarmac into the reception area, they almost forgot that this was a business arrangement and not a holiday.

Once out of the airport they found their hire car waiting and were soon on their way down the island. Carol smiled as they drove past Kolymbia. She never had returned the phone calls, and after the first couple of weeks they stopped. It would certainly seem strange going back to Koki Apartments again.

They parked the car in a side street off the square. They walked on through the village, and it seemed quite surreal, she the one to give directions to the usually confident Richie. Carol was pleased to see that they had an upstairs room on the other side of the patio. You could still see the sea, and the fishing boats and, as before, everything was fresh and clean.

****

'MANCHESTER? WHAT THE HELL are we going to Manchester for?' Simon asked Geoff when he saw the tickets.

'What's the problem? A ticket is a ticket. I suppose Grady did not think when he did the booking'. There was no Mr. Grady, but Geoff had to invent some story about a friend who had organised the trip. He could not mention Pete, the egg man from Margate!

'Some people forget we have an airport down here. He probably checked out Heathrow and it was far too expensive. Not that I have been on a plane for about twenty-five years, and then only over to Spain on a job. Anyway, he has booked assistance he said, so they meet you with a wheelchair and take you through. Takes half the time, and you get to go to the front of the queue. He did that last year when he took his mum to California to see his sister and the kids'.

'Bugger his sister, how are we to get to Manchester at eight-thirty in the morning?'

'A lot of help you are going to be if you can't work that one out. We get the train up the day before and stay in a hotel. Hardly rocket science'.

Even then Simon did not think there was any reason for concern. A night in a hotel with a 'full English' that he had not cooked himself! He would not argue with that. When Geoff first read the tickets, he thought the same as Simon. Pete had got the tickets and who Pete got them from, only God knows. Geoff did not ask questions.

With a bit of luck, he would get back the money he was owed, and maybe a bit more. And get a free trip to Greece. Though Geoff was old enough to know that very little in life is free.

Sy had other things on his mind for the next few days. He did not want any problems whilst he was away. He had rung around and pulled in a few favours. The supermarket would deliver anything at any time, he would settle the account when he got back, he told his guests. George would come over if a plumber was needed, Dave was his electrician, and all these phone numbers were on a large card pinned on the wall behind the desk. Any other problems and the Polish couple who had the B and B up the road would drop by to help. Everything was sorted, and then the days dragged by, even though Simon was busy, even this early in the season.

Now, a few last words with his guests, checking again that Geoff's luggage was within the right weight, not trusting him not to sneak something in at the last minute, and they were in the taxi to the station.

The train ride up north was a lot better than Simon had expected. Once across London, which they sensibly did by taxi, they were booked into first class. They had a drink, then a light meal, and after dosing off once or twice, they were in Crewe. Thankfully, they did not even have to change platforms to wait for the airport train, and less than an hour later they were in the Best Western Hotel, with their feet up and a whisky each, taken from the mini bar in the room.

Simon was up early, had his shower first, and went down for breakfast. Now he was in holiday mood, and able to laugh at Geoff's notion about cheaper air fares if you go from Manchester. 'Must be some discount if you add up the train and hotel', he had told him. But what the hell! The old boy could afford it, and if it was what he wanted, then why not?

Just as 'Grady' had said, once you told a girl at the desk you had booked assistance, a chap arrived with a wheelchair.

They went through private doors and along deserted passageways. When it came to checking-in at the security gate, the cord across the access was opened and they went through to the front of the queue. Only Geoff caused some amusement with his daft cockney humour.

'Can you tell me', he was addressing the young woman who was frisking him with a thing like a hairdryer. 'How I can smuggle diamonds through here'? Not that I have got any, but I am writing a book and I want to get the details right'.

The guy standing with his arms folded, but his eyes going in every direction, allowed a smirk to go across his face.

The lady with the hairdryer leaned a bit closer. 'If I knew that sir, I would not be doing this bloody job', she whispered to Geoff, in a Mancunian accent you could cut with a knife.

But when they got to the place where you pick up your shoes, belt, and mobile phone, that have been through the scanner, he asked again.

'Random checks, amazing what gets picked up with random checks', had been the informative reply.

The young chap who had pushed the wheelchair appeared again and took them down to the gate. There was a queue forming to show your boarding pass and passport but that was ignored. Straight to the desk and naturally people stood back to allow the wheelchair through. Simon felt a bit of a fraud walking through as well, but that is what he had been told to do, so he did not worry about it too much. Geoff had said he could do the steps and Simon took both small 'carry-on' bags. When Geoff turned to thank the lad, he passed him twenty quid 'for a drink'.

They had downed a couple of whiskeys already that morning, so for Geoff, the flight passed in a pleasant haze, only disturbed by the steward bringing the trolley with their meals.

But Simon was wide awake, mesmerized by the view from the window. He had just assumed that they would be flying so high that it would be only clouds. To see the mountains, and occasionally the villages, below them, took his breath away. Simon had not said anything to Geoff, but the truth was, he had never flown before. Yes, he had a passport, if you lived on the south coast there were always trips over the channel. Now this was everything he ever imagined. As they came in over Athens the sea shone like glass. Little boats bobbed about, and bigger cruise ships sailed majestically along, as if in slow motion.

Then the plane began to descend, turning in over the land, dipping slightly on one side. The sound of the engines changed, as houses and buildings rushed towards them. A slight bump and they had landed. The aircraft travelled quite a way on the tarmac before coming to a halt. People started to rush and push. The moment of fantasy was gone.

They had been told to wait until everyone else had left the cabin and that a platform had been organised for Geoff, to save him walking down the steps.

Once on the tarmac they expected the wheelchair, but none arrived. The guy who had helped with the hand luggage was about to walk away. 'Hold on mate', Simon called to him. 'What happens now'?

'Go in door', he replied indicating a glass door only about a hundred yards away. 'I have work to do', and he was on the platform with the doors closed, and with a clank of the machinery was driving away.

'Welcome to Greece', Simon told Geoff with a laugh. 'No good standing here all day so we might as well go straight through the glass doors', they both laughed at the old cockney joke.

There was no one left at the carousel, but their cases were standing on the floor nearby.

'You wait near the exit, and I will go back and fetch the cases', Simon suggested to Geoff. That done they looked around the arrivals area. One man stood there with a wheelchair and a sign in his hand.

'There's our man', Geoff said when he saw him.

'But it says MORRIS, not Marsham'.

'That's right, he's our man'.

And that was the first moment Simon realised that all was not as straight forward as Geoff had made it out to be. But he said nothing, for there was nothing he could think of to say.

****

It annoyed Simon that after all these years Geoff had not told him what the score was. More importantly not giving him a choice about being involved. Was he being paranoid? Was it that old habits die hard, and Geoff was only playing some game for bit of excitement? These days it was a stupid ruse.

'Kalimera, Mr. Morris. I'm instructed to take you to the Mystic Hotel sir', the driver informed them. 'I will take the cases first and put them in the car, then return to assist you'. And he did just that, all organised in a matter of minutes.

The drive from the airport was spectacular, one minute going through narrow streets where it would be hard to pass a bus. Then a wide junction, with traffic lights, a large white church, and supermarkets, obviously a village. And finally, along a coastal road with amazing views.

Simon had to admit that the English Channel, even on the hottest summer day, was never as blue as the sea he was driving past. He was not sure what he had expected, but certainly not dual carriageways. There were lots of massive hotels, all shiny white paint, and balconies. The taxi turned in away from the sea and under an archway. He did not know it, but they had now entered the medieval city.

The pavements were narrow, where they existed at all, and opened to a large square of shops and restaurants, they turned up hill, and then left off the main street. They stopped in a car park, tumble down buildings around them. Once out of the car, Simon had the chance to look around.

The buildings were made of stone with a great archway seeming to stand alone. On the skyline was the round dome of a church, well, he presumed it was a church and beyond that a tall tower, which looked like the Muslim 'call to prayer' towers he had seen in London. There was a restaurant with tables outside, and umbrellas to keep the tables shaded. And all the time he could feel the warm air, just as he had done when leaving the plane.

The driver took the two larger cases from the boot and asked them to follow him. They did not go to the restaurant but along the path. Once through a small door they entered a room of ancient stone and a floor made of pebbles. A sparkling bar was on the right-hand side and a low coffee table ahead with comfortable sofas. This area was framed by an archway and softly lit.

Theodosis Markoulis came towards them and introduced himself in perfect English.

'Good evening, sir. I am Theo, welcome to my hotel. I hope you had a comfortable journey. What may I offer you? A drink first or would you like to go to your rooms and settle in.

They both accepted the offer of a drink and sat in the armchairs.

The driver had returned with the hand luggage and addressed Geoff. 'Enjoy your visit to our island sir'.

'Thank you', Geoff replied, passing him twenty euro note.

They sat for about an hour in the small reception area, asking Theo about his hotel and Simon telling him about their guest house in Folkestone. 'Nothing as grand as this place, but I tell no lie, it is quite unique. And just the three rooms, as you have here'. Though if truth were told, as clean and comfortable as the Folkestone B and B was, it was nothing like the Mystic. But Simon was always open to new things, and one of the small, but important additions he had already noticed in the Mystic reception lounge, was the bookcase.

He addressed Theo. 'Do you know, it has never occurred to me to have a bookcase. People leave books behind, and I dump them on the landing for a week or two, but if there are too many, I bin them. Though I must say I hate doing that. But a bookcase would solve that problem. I will sort that when I get back. Thanks Mr.' Simon hesitated over the pronunciation of the Greek name.

'Theo, I much prefer Theo. I am pleased to have been of some help to you'.

Theo was far too polite to say that his bookcase contained many heavy tomes about the architecture and history of Rhodes, not a few unwanted paperbacks.

It was irrelevant if his guests were happy. And when he thought about it, perhaps Simon had raised a good point, perhaps he should have a 'holiday novel' bookshelf on the staircase. He would think about it, and perhaps ask his regular clientele if they would use such a facility.

But it had been a tiring day and the guests gratefully made their way to bed.

****

Breakfast was served in the small lounge where Theo had entertained them last night. They had only ordered Nescafé and croissants and found ample butter and marmalade on the table waiting for them. They had slept well, and taken their time getting up. But the sun was shining, and certainly Simon wanted to be out looking around.

'Those cowboy shirts that we are collecting from Symi Island', Geoff had begun.

'What cowboy shirts?' Simon asked.

'I ordered a couple on- line. From a leather shop on Symi'.

'You did? That was smart of you, when you tell me you have a problem working a mobile phone'.

'Well, I did not do it, I just said that looks a good idea, and the lad in the barber's shop did it all. I just paid for it, and we collect them. What's the problem?'

'What about them? Simon asked. He had no idea what Geoff was talking about. If cowboy shirts, or did he say jackets, had been mentioned, then he really could not remember the conversation at all.

'Well, I ordered fancy buttons, and we have to pick them up at a shop that has a button factory, by the Mandraki harbour'.

Thankfully, Theo came back in, to ask if everything was to their liking, and would they like more coffee. Having said 'yes thank you' and 'no thank you', Geoff asked about Mandraki.

'Oh, it is only a short walk, and easily managed with the wheelchair. If you do not mind waiting for about half an hour, I will gladly take you there', he offered.

Theo thought the best way was to go out of the Old Town, and onto the new wooden boardwalk, by the sea. Only a few cobble stones, and a very scenic stroll for anyone new to Rhodes. All the streets were full of tourists as a cruise ship had disgorged its passengers into the Old Town.

In some ways it was easier with the wheelchair, as people kindly moved out of the way. That is, once they realised that Simon and Geoff were waiting to pass through. Simon would have liked to stop and look around but was aware that Theo had given up his time to help them. They turned left again and out through an archway towards the sea. across the road, and onto the wooden walkway that followed the sea wall. Another left turn, through a small arch, and onto Mandraki harbour.

'Now I must leave you gentlemen', Theo told them. 'The shop you need is opposite the taxi rank. Once your business is settled, you can come back to this side and continue along to the end. There you will find a small café called Meltemi. It has lovely views over the sea to Turkey. But, if that is too far, then go down here, where the boats are moored. Enjoy your day'.

They thanked Theo for his help and set off to cross the road to the jewellery shop.

****

Panagiotis leaned back onto the stool behind the counter and waited.

There was adequate room for a wheelchair to negotiate into the shop. Simon was taking his time, admiring the glittering displays, wondering what was expensive, and what, if any, was just bling. He laughed to himself. He would not know the difference anyway.

Geoff was tapping onto the footrest. Simon stopped the chair and applied the brakes. Geoff stood up and took the few steps to the counter.

'Young man, I need to see the manager'.

Panagiotis was both curious and slightly apprehensive. He had already assumed that these were the clients he had been waiting for. Delivering a 'special parcel' did not happen often these days.

'Certainly sir, and how can I help you?'

'I've come to collect some buttons. It's a special order to take to Symi', Geoff explained,

Panagiotis was already wearing protective gloves. It was unusual for special parcels to come via the shop now, but he kept strictly to the old rules, nothing changed.

'And your business card sir? I would not want to give you the wrong package.'

'Oh, sorry mate, nearly forgot', and Geoff handed over the card Pete had given him.

'I understand that the account has already been paid', Geoff told him, hoping it had and there would be no complications.

'Certainly. Thank you, sir, for your custom and enjoy the rest of your holiday Mr. Morris'.

Panagiotis waited until they had left the shop. He opened his phone.

'Job done. But count me out next time. Not interested any more'.

****

Geoff did not really have a clue as to what he had collected. Why there was so much fuss about this small brown paper parcel. But he had the 'buttons' now, and that was all that mattered.

They went back to the harbour, and Simon pushed Geoff along the paved footpath. The view was amazing and the sea a clear blue that you did not see often in Folkstone.

Meltemi was right on the sea front It was too early for lunch so hey ordered a cold coffee, with a whiskey to pour into it.

An hour later and they were retracing their steps along the esplanade. You could not get lost Simon thought, as the sea was on one side and the town on the other. He said nothing but was relieved to see traffic lights ahead and people crossing and going into the town.

They came to a square with a fountain in the middle and stopped for a moment to look at the pigeons drinking from it. There were stone seahorses decorating the bowl. They moved on and were into another square with a fountain. A tall smart looking young man was standing outside an imposing looking restaurant. A menu page in his hand.

'Excuse me young feller', Geoff addressed him. 'Can you tell me where I can change some money around here?'

Aleksandros wished he had a euro for every time he had been asked that. Next to the Archipelagos restaurant where he worked was the Bureau de Change, with a large clear sign inside the glass fronted office, stating just that.

'It is here behind you sir', he politely replied. 'Thanks', said Geoff, thinking he was right in guessing that the lad was not Greek. But nothing was further than the truth. Alek was born in the village of Koskinou, only a few kilometres from the town. He had lost track of the years he had been working for Thanasis at the Archipelagos. What confused tourists was his immaculate English. Some asked if he was Australian, recognising an occasional twang.

Alek had been taught English as a child by his aunts. They had been born in Australia but returned to their family home in Koskinou. They opened a private school teaching English, and naturally Aleksandros was a willing pupil. Added to that he had spent several years speaking to English tourists.

He chatted to Geoff whilst Simon went to change some pounds to euros.

'Are you stopping for lunch sir or just a cold beer?' He asked. Simon was back and they agreed to stay for lunch.

'Nothing too foreign' Geoff told Alek.' But those beers in the big glasses look good'. Geoff had seen a couple on another table drinking from large glass boots and was certainly not going to miss that.

Then may I suggest our mixed grill for two. Always enjoyed by our English guests'.

Simon and Geoff were not disappointed. They could not finish all the beer but left little of their gigantic grill untouched. They thanked the waiter and Alek in Geoff's usual generous way and asked directions back to the Mystic hotel.

But, at the front of Geoff's mind was the thought of the job he was there to do, and would he pull it off, and be free for the next few years. Such thoughts had never bothered him before. He presumed it was all part of getting old.

They slept for the rest of the afternoon, only waking up in time to have a shower, and out to a nearby fish restaurant that Theo had recommended. After their meal they spent the evening sitting in the warm evening air with an iced drink, listening to the music. At the hotel they said 'good night' to Theo as they came through the reception area and went straight up to their room. Neither could remember the last time they were in bed before ten.

****

Geoff and Simon had decided on a leisurely day, not venturing further than along the harbour. This time they went to Kontiki. It was a large boat floating in the water. They were soon seated by the window looking out over the harbour to the sea. Simon ordered a frappe each and two whiskeys. This had become their holiday tipple. The sun shone, as it would shine every day from now till September. Not that they would be there in September, but that is what they had been told by Theo when at breakfast.

Theo also had details of their trip over to Symi island. The taxi driver had called in late last night.

'He will collect you just after eight this evening and take you down to the harbour. The boat taking you to is called the Yellow Submarine. The crew thought you might enjoy a trip around the harbour first, then when the regular tourists have left, they will nip you down to Lindos.'

'But we are going to Symi'. Not often that Geoff would open his mouth at the wrong time and place.

'I am sorry. If there is some mistake, I have the taxi number. I will call them and confirm the arrangements.'

'No, no, it is my mistake. We go to Symi another day'.

'Are you sure now. I am pleased you are going over to the island. It is beautiful there'.

Geoff was not sure he needed a sightseeing tour of Rhodes by night, but it was all out of his hands. He thanked Theo for the information.

'Are we coming back here after the island trip'? Simon had asked Geoff when enjoying a second drink.

'Not sure, so I expect we need to take all our gear with us. You would think they would give us a schedule, but it was cheap and cheerful, so what can you expect'.

'Certainly, the place we are in now is not cheap and cheerful, not a posh gaff like the Mystic', Simon pointed out. Geoff apologised to Theo. 'Sorry, Simon is right, I just meant the whole package was not expensive. We did not expect to be staying in a five-star hotel like this, and in the medieval city'.

Theo said he understood completely.

They packed their bags and lay on the beds for a siesta. The heat was getting to them both. They slept longer than intended, and only had time for a giro from a nearby café before their transport arrived.

****

Geoff assured Abu that he could walk the short distance from the quay on to the boat, and the wheelchair was carefully stowed, as were their cases. There were about twenty passengers, and Simon recognised a couple he had seen before, earlier in the day in Meltemi. It did not seem unusual to him, as he presumed most people staying in Rhodes would be doing the same tourist trips.

The view of the medieval city by night was stunning, and then to top it all they went below deck for the illuminated feeding of fish. Simon was not sure that it was real and not just a video, so he made a thumbs up sign to the diver and got a hand signal back, with a smile.

It did not take long to return to Mandraki, and the tourists started to disembark. The nice couple waited to let them go first but Geoff thanked them, suggesting go ahead, as he had a wheelchair to unload.

Everyone safely off and the crew went into action. The booking desk was closed. Ropes were unhooked again and within a few minutes the Yellow Submarine was making its way out of the harbour. Christos had told them about the passengers they were taking to Lindos, but as it was his birthday next day, the crew took the opportunity to turn the trip into a party.

He did wonder at first why everyone was on board including Abu, Dimitra, Maria and Christian. Naturally, Antony, Theodonis and Elisavet could not be left behind, as it would be difficult to get to Lindos without them.

Everyone introduced themselves and opened cans of beer for their guests. Soon the best of a Greek messe was spread on the table in the centre of the deck. As they had not eaten a proper meal that evening, Geoff and Simon were pleased to be asked to 'tuck in'. For a few moments Geoff forgot about the buttons in his jacket pocket. He was enjoying Greek hospitality at its best, and a light summer breeze as they headed out to sea, was making the trip comfortable.

Carol could not understand why Richie had suddenly turned moody. What more did he want? A lovely evening, a boat trip, a bar overlooking the harbour. Eventually he spoke.

'I was trailing the guy in the wheelchair. So how did I miss them getting off the boat. The esplanade was reasonably clear except some French people. But as soon as they had gone by, there was no sign of the English guys,' he told her in an unusual burst of sharing his work information.

'But they did not get off. I spoke to the crew, the tall black guy; reminded him that they were still on the boat. He told me he was taking them to Lindos this evening. There is another boat waiting to take them over to Symi Island'.

Ritchie leant forward and kissed her. His smile said it all.

****

Once the birthday supper had been cleared away and their boss given good wishes for the next year and beyond, the crew chatted quietly, or checked their phones. After all, they had been working all day.

Soon the lights of Palestra glowed in the dark. The Yellow Submarine drove up onto the beach. For many years there had been a small pier there. But it was never repaired and eventually it was unsafe and dismantled. Now everyone was saying goodbye, and the wheelchair had been opened and Geoff asked to sit in it. Between them the crew hoisted him and the chair onto dry land. Simon jumped off and their cases were placed nearby.

As the submarine pulled away a man came down some nearby steps to help them. Nicolas Nefeli owned the beach side Nefeli restaurant. He introduced himself.

'It is unusual for me to be here in Lindos these days', he told them. 'I have business interests in Rodos and my daughter Marianne manages the restaurant. But why are we talking here? Come up to the bar and we can relax with a drink'. It was only a few yards up the tarmac path and into the Nefeli. Even in the dark Simon could see it was not like any other place he had seen on Rhodes. There was an area of small tables at one side, but the umbrellas were of bamboo, giving the space a tropical island feel. On the far side were more formal dining tables, which Simon presumed correctly, were for groups. He did not consider wedding parties as he had no idea that hosting such events was one of their specialities.

'In a few moments, the pleasure boat 'Melani' will be here. They will take you safely over to

Symi. But you will have a drink with me first. It is quite safe to leave your bags here. This is Lindos, not a problem.

They sat in the semi darkness, whiskey in hand. They could be on a Hawaiian island Simon thought, admiring the umbrella over his head. But the truth was that the whiskey, added to the generous amounts of alcohol consumed on the submarine, left him not knowing or caring where he was.

It was twenty minutes later they saw the large boat coming towards the beach. Geoff did wonder how it was going land but had now been in Greece long enough to know that there is a way round everything. So, he was not surprised that the Melani just came straight onto the sand, no bother at all.

He could see the captain, Yannis, on the deck. But it was the first officer, Angelos, who had leapt off the boat and onto the beach, rope in hand.

Naturally, they did not leave straight away. They were greeted by Nicolas, and after a few exchanges of local news in Greek, they spoke English again. And another drink was poured.

Yannis and Angelos enjoyed relaxing. They had been busy all day. Not only their regular day trip, out from Lindos harbour, but also a wedding party from St. Pauls Bay to Nefeli.

'Don't the girls get their feet wet'? Geoff asked. The men laughed. 'Not a problem. We have a step ladder for them to reach the beach. Everything is well organised', Angelos replied. As usual Simon marvelled at the command of English. He could trace a feint accent. But he would not have guessed that Angelos' mother, Melanie, was from Northern Ireland. Never entered his mind.

Now it was time to leave. They thanked Nicolas, and Geoff in his usual way offered to pay. He was politely told to keep his money in his pocket. The cases and the wheelchair were loaded, and Geoff was assisted up the step ladder. The engines started, and dozing off in comfortable chairs, at last they were on the way to Symi.

If Yannis thought it unusual to be taking two Englishmen over to Symi, late at night, and from

Pallas beach, then he did not waste much time thinking about it. It never ceased to amaze him what English tourists would do! And the price offered for this easy trip was more than enough to compensate for the extra work.

****

SIMON AND GEOFF DID NOT see the beautiful harbour, and the painted houses rising high above the cliffs. That would be for another day. Their leave taken of Yannis and Angelos, they were at last on Symi Island.

The buttons Geoff was carrying in his inside pocket were nearly burning into him. He just wanted to get into the leather shop and deliver them. Then pick up the shirts and leave. He presumed that would have to be for another day, as he doubted it would be open now. Would there be a taxi waiting for them as promised?

The taxi driver was leaning against his Mercedes, a cigarette in hand. There was only one man with a wheelchair on the quay, so no problem identifying his passenger. And as there was only one taxi on the quayside, Simon steered Geoff towards the car.

Geoff was surprised to see lights on along the harbour. The many tourist gift shops were busy restocking their shelves. He rammed the brakes on the chair and stood up.

'Wait here, I have to call in a shop, just wait'. Simon was surprised. It was unlike Geoff to be rude to anyone. "There it is', Geoff waved his hand in the direction of Takis leather shop. 'You wait with the taxi', he told Simon.

Geoff introduced himself as Jim Morris. He showed the card. It only took a second or two to hand over the buttons, as the man was obviously expecting them.

'And you are a friend of Petros, tell him I miss him. We had some good nights out together, many years ago now'. Geoff was furious.

'No, I do not know him. I am here to collect a parcel. Do you have it now'.

Takis started to laugh. 'You English, always yesterday you need something. How can the garments be ready when you only bring me the buttons now? Call back in two days.'

'I thought it would all be sorted quicker than that', Geoff told him rudely. 'Two days' was the curt reply, so Geoff made his way out of the shop.

They were hardly back in the taxi than they were getting out again. Barely a couple of hundred yards along the road, and now they were entering Lapetos Village. It was, Simon thought, like a conservation area you might find in a national park in England, though of course it was nothing like anything you would find in England. What struck him most were the colours. Even in the dark you could see tangerine walls, with white trims to the windows. A lovely custard colour on another little house, with dark green shutters. Then, a blue house, a deep-sea blue, and terracotta tiles on the roof. Outside every little place was a private sitting area, and on the upper floor, a balcony.

Geoff was just standing, speechless, leaning on the taxi door. Certainly, he had never seen anything like it before.

The driver had gone into the reception area to say that they had arrived. A dark-haired young woman came out with him, and with Geoff now sitting in the wheelchair, they entered the door of the custard- coloured house.

The first thing Simon noticed was the bed. A black metal frame, normal enough, but the size was something else. Gigantic. He looked around for the second bed, but that was it, though there was an eight- foot sofa. There were two wardrobes, a kitchenette for making tea or a snack, a small table with chairs, and a French door leading out onto a veranda. And the walls of the room were also coloured. A sort of muted tone of the scene outside. And it was immaculate. Absolutely one hundred per cent immaculate.

'Our place at home will be in for a refit when we get back, that is for certain. New curtains, bedspreads with some colour, not painting the walls till next spring, but no more magnolia for me', he told Geoff.

'If one of you would kindly come over to the reception desk later, with both passports, and sign in, that would be fine', the young lady told them.

'Well, I know where I am sleeping, you can sort yourself out'. Geoff told Simon.

'I'm sleeping with you Daddy, I want to sleep in the big bed', Simon replied.

What Geoff told him is not printable, but the two men started to laugh until they were choking, and coughing, but the foul mood Geoff had felt in the leather shop had lifted.

'I need a drink', Geoff managed to say. 'Then we had better go and get one', Simon suggested. 'Once I have checked us both in as the lady asked'. He found the desk and the paperwork was done without a problem. He managed not to show any reaction to the name on Geoff's passport. He could laugh about such nonsense now.

'I don't need that bloody chair, everything looks to be close by', Simon was told and still laughing they walked together down towards the garden area.

Geoff was beginning to feel some relief from the tension he had been under since Pete the egg man had first asked him about going to Greece, nearly three months ago. Now they had two days in this amazing place, pick up the shirts or waistcoats whatever the man had said they were, and head back to the Mystic.

They came to the pool. So, a swimming pool is a swimming pool, but not this one. It had a roof over it, but no walls. Only stone arches. It was curved, with a paved area made of the same pebbles as were in the Mystic, with the black ones set into the others in designs of leaves and flowers. The sunbeds were just outside for people who wished to sunbathe. And Palm trees and potted plants.

But they headed on to find the bar. Maybe swim tomorrow.

****

Next morning, Carol and Richie were on the early hovercraft to Symi. They were pleased with their studio at the Nereus. It was right on the harbour and had a balcony looking onto the sea. But the view could not be more different from their Koki rooms. The harbour was quite a deep curve, and, as they followed the sea wall around, pastel painted houses rose from the sea to the sky.

And it was only a few doors away from the leather shop. Richie still had no idea what he was looking for. But if he had to sit on a Greek island, checking who went in or out of some place, to be honest, he could not care less.

Carol was over the moon. Once they had taken their tooth paste out of their travel bag, and done a few other necessary, but not important things, she was off out.

She wandered along the sea front, then over a small bridge. There were more shops and side streets there, and she wanted to get out of the sun. Just like Lindos, every twist and turn brought something new to see. Little cafes where the space outside was twice as big as inside. Large padlocked wrought iron gates, leading into a spacious garden of pine trees and yuccas. Cats of every colour sat on the doorsteps.

Richie reported back to the office via his phone. 'They were picked up on a private boat going to Symi yesterday. Will check out a few nearby bars later. Will be surprised if anything comes from this. Yes, Sir, I agree, whole job is a bit off the wall'. No way was he going to mention losing them on Mandraki. What difference would it make, he was here on Symi now.

On the way back from her walk, Carol saw the Chinese restaurant, and fancied eating there that evening. But now she was getting tired, and an afternoon nap was a luxury she could never afford at home. So, once in the studio, after making tea for them both, she lay on the bed and slept.

****

As inviting as the swimming pool looked, neither Simon nor Geoff went swimming the next morning. After a lazy breakfast, they walked around the harbour. They did not take the wheelchair as there were plenty of benches to sit on, and every second shop was a café, making it easy for Geoff to rest if he needed to.

At one end of the harbour, they rounded a corner to another small bay. Out of the breeze now, Geoff chose a café table looking out to sea. Simon ordered lunch.

'Two chicken giro platters please, and a can of lager each', Simon told the young waitress, but when the order arrived, he realized one plate would have been plenty for them to share.

'Somehow the salad tastes different here', Geoff commented. And Simon knew that his friend must be feeling good, as picking fault with food was a sign when Geoff was unwell.

They wandered back to their accommodation, and stretched out on the beds, they dosed off. Well Simon did, but Geoff was too anxious, and stayed alert.

There was a knock on the door. It was the young lady from reception. She told Geoff there was a man waiting in the foyer with a parcel for him.

He quickly put his shoes on and walked briskly along the corridor. His knee felt good, he was sure the sun had helped.

Takis extended his hand. 'I apologise, it was wrong of me to speak of our friend yesterday. I was just pleased to know he was well. But I should know better than to make a personal remark when on a business transaction. Here are the goods you ordered. Any problem please see me this evening. I will be at the shop till eleven p.m. and there again in the morning just after ten'.

Geoff took the parcel from Takis.

'It is difficult for me to talk to you alone so may I suggest we find a room to unpack and examine the goods'.

Geoff knew he was out of his depth, as he had no idea what he was collecting, except it was 'country and western' gear. But he was not going to let Takis know that.

That Takis had no notion of the value of the buttons on the shirt or the number of diamonds on the 'rhinestone cowboy' panels he had used for the back of the waist coats, would have surprised Geoff.

They opened one parcel. Geoff picked up the shirt first. It was a heavy cream linen. There were pearl buttons down the front and on the tabs of the collar. Around the pearls were glittery bits, perhaps crystal he thought. Takis took the shirt and turned it around. Along the yoke at the back were more pearls and purple glass bits. Quite amazing.

The shirt was folded back in the packaging and Takis lifted out a waistcoat. The leather was a mustard colour and exceptionally soft. The same buttons down the front as the shirt. But on the back was 'rhinestone cowboy' picked out in those glittery glass bits.

'This looks fine, I am not the expert, but I do not think it could be improved. Is the other one the same? He asked Takis.

'The other shirt is tan coloured and the waistcoat cream, the buttons are a different style. Shall I get it out for you'?

'No, no need for that. Do you want me to sign for them?'.

Takis took a phone from his pocket.

'No need, our conversations are all on here. Everything is covered'.

Geoff was not sure if he liked the sound of that, but too late now to disagree. And it was as much in Takis' interest to be discreet as it was in his.

He thanked him, and they shook hands. Takis returned to his leather shop on the harbour,

Geoff went quietly back to his room, pleased to find Simon still fast asleep.

Both Takis and Geoff thought about the transaction they had been involved in during the past few days, and both silently vowed that this would be the last of their shady dealing. Yes, the last time.

****

The return ferry would not leave Symi till late in the afternoon, so they had a leisurely start in the morning.

'Another nice day', Geoff remarked when he joined Simon at the breakfast table.

'Yes, seems strange when you are used to always wondering what the weather will be like in the morning. Nice place this, seems a shame to be leaving'.

'We could always come back again, but I have some business to do in Rhodes town this next week'.

Here comes the dodgy bit, what is the old bugger up to now. Must be something substantial by the money he has laid out so far, Simon though, but still said nothing.

The view looking back to the island of Symi was more spectacular than when they had arrived in the dark. The sun sparkled on the water, and the pastel houses, piled high on top of each other, looked more like a picture book than reality.

'Wish I had the money years ago to come to places like this', Simon said to no one in particular, as he leaned over the rail.

'You and me both'.

Carol had been standing nearby and heard the comment.

'Hello again, are you going back as well then'? More a statement than a question as they were out to sea already.

'Yes, seems that way. Mind you the place we stay on Rhodes, down in Lindos, is spectacular, just quite different'.

So, the copper is off somewhere else, just a coincidence them being on the boat again.

'Well, enjoy the rest of your holiday. Better get back to my friend down in the café, nice talking to you'.

Geoff had poured a whisky into his frappe and very tasty it was too. He was pleased with his visit to the island, he had what he had come for. The new buttons were safely on the shirts. Everything looked Kosher.

A car was waiting at the harbour to meet the ferry. Not the same driver, this one was English. They did not go back to the Mystic as Simon had expected but were off down the island.

Another spectacular drive, sometimes on the coastal road and then past villages nestled in the inland valleys. And the hotels! They just got bigger and better as they went along. He wondered where they would be staying and if it would have a pool. He was surprised how green everything was, considering the lack of rain. Now he had forgotten about Geoff's business and was enjoying the drive just as a regular tourist would.

****

PART 7

IN PYLONA VILLAGE Sue and Pete were curious, but most of all delighted. They both considered an empty house a rather sad sight. The house had been sitting empty for the best part of six years. It was vacant and overgrown, a silent witness that someone's dream of life on a Greek island had come to a sticky end. Had they separated? Had the banks foreclosed?

So, it was a surprise, when they saw a 'garden renovation' van park outside the neglected house and two men, with chain saws and a rotavator, began work on the garden.

A few days later, a furniture van arrived from the shop in Archangelos. Mattresses and sofas were taken out and new ones put in. Sue thought that a good clean to remove dust and cobwebs should have been on the agenda. It had been, but they had missed that part of the renovation when out shopping in Rhodes town the day before. By the end of the next week packages and bed linen arrived and, they assumed, that a family would soon be moving in.

But they were wrong, because the new owner was Geoff, accompanied, so everyone assumed, by his son.

To anyone else, a three- bedroom, detached villa, in a quiet cul de sac in a select Greek village, would have been a vision of heaven. But it was not what Geoff had wanted. First, he had no ambition to live on a Greek island, and more importantly, no wish to own anything that might connect him to any dodgy deal. If fact, he was beginning to have twinges of regret at getting involved in this game at all. Bit late now. All he needed was the ten grand he had been promised for his part in delivering the collection of gems he had brought back from Symi. And if possible, the ten owed to him by Ben Jenkins for a dodgy job almost ten years ago. That was what he came for and that, would have done the trick for him. No fuss, and no bother passing the goods on to Pete the egg man once they got back. Not a lot he could do about any of it now, so he decided to just sit back and enjoy the sunshine. He had not signed anything yet, so no one could link him to the house, not legally anyway. Also, it might be the last holiday he would get at his age, particularly if the job went wrong on him. So, he had decided to make the most of it.

For Simon, who had only expected a couple of rooms, or a small apartment, it was a gift. A spacious house with a garden and a pool was, he considered, a bit of a lottery win. And there were a couple of bars and cafes nearby. Too far from the sea? Not at all, he had lived just a two-minute walk from the beach for most of his life, albeit the English Channel, and they had the hire car outside the front door. So, a trip to some place called Lindos, where Geoff wanted to go to some posh restaurant, was no problem.

At the back of his mind was this nagging doubt about why they were there, but so far, he could not find any valid reason to assume it was anything other than a holiday. And that copper and his wife being on Symi island? Well, even they are allowed holidays. Not a holiday his wife had said, but something to do with refugees. Not that Simon had seen or heard anything about refugees himself, but he had seen the pictures of the poor kids, on the news last year.

'Do you want another top up Geoff, or are we going out for one', he called out to his friend who was on the sun lounger in the back porchway. But Geoff had dozed off, and a few snores was the only reply. But that did not stop Simon pouring himself another scotch and coke, with ice. He took his mobile out with him, just to check there were no messages from the Guest house, or his daughters anxious to know how he was.

No messages. So, his glass safely on the side table, he sat back on the lounger, with his feet up, and enjoyed the warm evening air.

****

CAROL WAS A BIT MIFFED. Richie was supposed to be attending an international conference about the refugee situation. But, up till now he had not been to any meetings. Certainly, the phone seemed to go non-stop, and whoever he had been talking to spoke Italian. He had been off on a small boat twice, but she had not been invited along. So, except for the days they had spent on Symi, she had done nothing but sit up on the balcony and read her book. Well, not quite true, they had been out to eat every evening. But Richie was not really relaxed. She was disappointed for him. He was very much an outdoors sort of guy, and he was not swimming or walking. Just on the balcony with her, pretending to read. Though she knew he was not, as every time a boat came or went into that little harbour, he picked up his binoculars. And then made notes. The only thing of any consequence was the late lunch they were invited to at Mavrikos in Lindos.

Everyone was very polite to her, speaking English when possible. And the food was amazingly good. But as soon as the discussion got heated the language was Greek, or Italian. To her surprise the nice chap Carol had spoken to, on the boat going to Symi, was there on another table with his father in the wheelchair. They were with some Greek friends, who were talking loudly, as Greek men do.

'I think it is a good deal for you. If you do not want to come here yourself, then you can rent it out'.

Simon was not quite sure what the conversation was about. Was Geoff thinking of buying the house in Pylona? A bit in the sticks and he could never manage to live there on his own, even with the help of those lovely people next door.

'Bit of a long way to come and change the sheets on a Friday', he added. At least that was something he did know about. He got strange looks from the Greeks, then they went off into a row, or at least it sounded like a row, in their own language.

'Enjoy your holiday. Our friend will call and see you when back in England. Then you will have time to decide. But it is a good offer', the quieter, more smartly dressed man added. And that seemed to be the end of the conversation, more wine was ordered, and they sat back admiring the view. Once their glasses were empty the men stood, and shaking hands all round, made their way out to the square.

Carol came over to say hello to Simon, and he introduced her to Geoff.

'Flipping heck, it is hard work here trying to have a chat with this lot. They talk so fast and so loud. Give me the local bar along Chiswick Reach any time', Carol told them, and both men agreed.

They laughed, and although Geoff offered her a glass of wine and a chair, she declined. 'Best get back to the old man', she told them. On that note they parted company.

Geoff found that the bill had been paid, so they also left Mavrikos.

Simon still had not got a clue as to why they had gone there in the first place. He hoped that Geoff would not suggest going again, although the food had been out of this world, and the wine first class.

Carol and Richie walked hand in hand back to the apartment. Along the back turnings of Lindos they chatted about more domestic things. Did he need any more T shirts? and why not take the chance to buy some handmade leather sandals whilst they were in the village. But he declined both offers. He suggested Carol go next morning to Archangelos and treat herself to a couple of new sundresses.

'No thank you, I am quite happy here in Lindos. There are plenty of clothes shops if shopping was what I wanted to do.   Carol and Richie were once again out on the Koki balcony, overlooking the sea, watching the little boats bobbing around in the dark harbour below. It was calm and peaceful, and he thought what a fool he had been, not to be taking Carol on proper holidays to places like this. They had possibly another week in Lindos, so he had been informed, but he promised himself he would be back. Nothing to do with work, just a week away, like most couples did.

Next morning Carol was on the balcony, with a coffee and her book. After all they spent so little time together in the normal working week, and she had just had an amazing holiday, here in Lindos. She was quite content.

There must be something she could organise for Richie. She knew that he was officially working, but surely not twenty-four-seven. Book a boat trip perhaps? No, Richie needed something more than that. She remembered seeing information about the diving school. Now that would be a treat he would enjoy. Face book would have the answers, maybe go on the 'From Lindos with Love' page? Bound to be some info there.

****

IT WAS BERYL AND ROY, the English couple living across the road from the Pylona villa, who invited Simon and Geoff to join the evening boat trip.

'It is not really a tourist trip, as most of the people will be Brits who live here. But I rang Pat Allen who organises it and there are a few places left'. Beryl had explained to Pat that probably Simon and Geoff had not gone on any boats, except the ferry to Symi, because of having to manage the wheelchair. She agreed that there would be plenty of lads willing and able to get the chair on and off, both in Lindos and Haraki. So not a problem.

Simon thanked Beryl and Geoff insisted on paying for all the fares. Once that was sorted, Simon told Geoff that they were going on a mystery trip. Neither of them had a clue where to find Haraki.

'Must be some spot along the coast if we are going by boat', said Geoff, rather stating the obvious.'

Roy knocked the door two days later to say they would be leaving at six o'clock. 'I've cleaned the boot out, so plenty of room for the chair. You will need jackets as it gets quite breezy on the way back'.

Geoff thought they should wear the cowboy shirts they had brought back from Symi. 'After all, we do not go out that often. You never know, there might be other country and western fans on the boat, and it would be a good conversation piece'.

Simon thought they were a bit flash for a boat trip, but it did not bother him one way or the other. If it made Geoff happy, then why not?

The 'Western gear' was much admired by Roy and Beryl. It was many years since they had belonged to a club and had the full regalia. Happy memories of a different way of life before they moved to Greece.

Driving to Lindos, where they would board the boat, took about half an hour. The slope down to the pier, at the end of the small Lindos beach, was quite steep, but manageable with both Roy and Simon holding the wheelchair handle. By the time he had reached the boat, Simon was wishing he had not bothered with a shirt at all.

Getting the chair on was easy enough, and they found a place to sit. It was very much like a social club outing, as everyone chatted away. When talking to Simon or Geoff, everyone told them how long they had been on the island, and where they had bought their house. Geoff played along, telling all about the ten-year lease on the Pylona villa. There was a bar, and they had a couple of beers, whilst watching the coast outlined in the evening light. Eventually they pulled into a small pier at Haraki. Roy and Beryl took them along the crowded, café lined esplanade, to a restaurant at the quieter end. They ordered and ate a luscious meal of lamb chops and oven potatoes, with a side salad, and a bottle of red wine to share.

Simon raised his glass, 'To a great view, good food, and excellent company'. Roy and Beryl replied 'yia mas', which he presumed meant 'cheers.' What an enjoyable evening.

The sun had gone down, and it was getting a little chilly. Now everyone was making their way to the boat, and soon they were all on their way back to Lindos.

Miles Davis rarely went on this event, as he only lived up the hill, inland from Haraki, at Kalathos.

He usually just joined everyone at the bar when they arrived. But this evening was different. His mother, Shirley, had fancied the boat trip; it would give her the chance to catch up with the many friends she had not seen during the busy summer.

Miles had met Simon last week in the Lindos 404 bar, so when they bumped into each other on the return trip it was a 'hello mate, how are you' situation.

'Where did you get the gear?' Miles asked him. 'Can't say I have seen many shirts like that around here'.

'Symi island, the leather shop on the harbour', Simon replied. 'But the glittery bits are a one off, done to order'. Simon swung around to give Miles a better look at the embellishment on the back. But it was the cuffs that had caught Mile's eye. Long, with six buttons, large buttons almost looking like cuff links. He had certainly not seen that styling before. On the points of the collar were metal claps, or maybe they were sewn on, but each one was studded with rhinestones.

'Here try it on, should be about your size', Simon suggested to Miles. They laughed as they swapped shirts. Certainly, Miles' purple silk was an exclusive retro style.

At that moment Roy came over to Simon and whispered 'Your friend needs the bathroom. I said I would help him down the stairs, but he said to call you'.

By the time they had come back up on to the deck the boat had pulled into the pier at Lindos. Simon looked around for Miles but could not see him. He saw a man that Miles had been talking to. Taking off Mile's purple shirt he asked him 'Would you please give this back to Miles for me? Tell him I will see him in the 404 during the week. Thanks.' 'No problem', the guy replied.

But there was a problem!

Some five minutes earlier Miles had taken the shirt off to return it to Simon, it was folded onto the rail.

It had only taken a second. Shirley had waited till most people had gone down the steps. Even so, she slipped on the decking, and without a moment's hesitation Miles had moved forward to assist his mother. She was not hurt, and he had long ago given up asking why she did not wait for him to help her.

It had only taken a second, maybe two. One gust of wind and the precious garment had gone. It had bobbed around, then disappeared. It was nowhere to be seen. Just a drop in the ocean.

****

At lunch time the following day Simon and Geoff were on their way up to the Pylona Arms for a pint and a snack. Geoff had said he was fed up with the chair, and his knee felt much better after resting on the sunbed. As they passed the end of the road Peter Moore was chatting to a man they had seen once or twice, but not yet met.

After the 'kalimera' greeting Peter introduced them to Lee O'Flynn.

'Lee runs a diving school here, well not from Pylona, but all around the island. Are you into diving at all?'

'Oh, been ducking and diving all my life', was Geoff's quick reply.

'I've heard that one a few times', Lee told him, but laughing at the joke anyway.

'Not for me I'm afraid, but what about you Simon. Ever tried diving?' he asked.

'Fancied it, but never got around to it. And I've lived near the sea all my life', Simon told them.

'Well, now's your chance. Make a change from pushing me up and down the place. Not been much of a holiday for you, has it?

'If you do decide to go with Waterhoppers for the day, then you, Geoff, can spend the day with us. Sue loves having visitors to cook for. Or if I am not working, we can go off out somewhere. Is that a deal?' Peter asked.

They agreed for Lee to let them know when and where, and the group parted company. They enjoyed their salad with sardines, and a couple of cans of Mythos. Back to the house and a laze on the sunbeds, and the day was almost gone.

Geoff found the walk and lunch was enough for one day, and only wanted a baguette for supper. Simon needed to go into Lindos, to find Miles and retrieve his shirt. He hitched in without any problems, not wanting to take the hire car in the dark and knew Miles would drop him back later. But Miles was not in the 404 and no one had seen him that evening. Robert and Pat offered him a lift home, as they lived in Vlicha anyway. He explained to them about the shirt. 'Oh, you have no need to worry, could not be in safer hands', Pat told him. 'Do you need a phone number, or shall I ring him in the morning and say you were looking for him?'

Simon thought the last suggestion was the better idea, he thanked them for the lift, and waved goodbye.

Geoff had already gone to bed. Simon poured himself a glass of coke, added some ice, and sat out in the garden. There was that velvet darkness that is hard to find in England, where streetlights blaze out into the sky.

We could sell up the house at home and open a holiday place here. B and B is the same in any country. Old Geoff seems happy with this place, and the neighbours, well, could not get better. Wonder what it is like in the winter? With that thought he made his way to bed.

Early next morning Miles was knocking on the door, but to Simon's surprise he did not have the shirt with him. Simon invited him in, made a coffee and they sat outside overlooking the pool, and beyond that, the field of olive trees.

After a few minutes of casual banter, Simon could wait no longer.

'Got the 'cowboy' thing mate?' he asked.

'I am sorry to say I have not. It blew over the rail, into the sea just as we were leaving the boat last week. I have been over to Takis, on Symi island, described the shirt, and asked if he would make a new one. He said it would take a while, as he would have to order more material in. But the decoration was a one off and once I had the shirt would have to find an artisan to decorate it. So, I have ordered, and paid for it. Be ready in about a week. He will deliver it over to Rhodes. He said something about special buttons, but I said not to worry, you could sort that out later. Sorry mate'.

Thankfully, Geoff was still in bed enjoying a lazy morning, and heard nothing of Mile's news.

Simon thanked him for the trouble he had gone to. They agreed to meet up in the 404 later in the week.

Miles drove back to Kalathos

What a lot of fuss for a bloody cowboy shirt, and if it is not here by the time we leave, I can ask Miles to post it over. Better see if Geoff wants a fry up, will be almost lunch time if we wait any later.

****

PART 8

RUTH AND BERTIE HAD fallen back into their earlier routine, well almost.

They still enjoyed dinner at Medeast most weeks and a home cooked supper on Thursdays. But some weekends, instead of going out down the island they were going up to Rhodes town and looking at apartments. Bertie could have stayed in the Greek Air Force club, near the Church, or at the exclusive Mystic hotel in the Old Town. But he chose a small studio between the pink Mosque and St. Georges bastion owned by an old friend Stergos. Naturally, they went to Romeo's for dinner. It was an ideal location from which to search for a flat.

Bertie had set his heart on the Old Town, and they wandered up and down the back streets, armed with his mobile phone, looking for places with rental signs and telephone numbers.

The following weekend they were walking the streets again.

'I thought I knew my way around', Bertie confessed to Ruth after a particularly long afternoon. 'But there are whole sections of the town I never knew existed. And if I wanted to go back to a certain area again, I doubt I could find my way'.

They had stopped once again, and were sitting in the courtyard of Auvergne café, near the Freedom gate, when Josephine, the Savaidis coach escort came in. Bertie waved and invited her to join them. Once the initial greeting was over Bertie mentioned about his search for an apartment.

'Wait here and I will talk to Mikez. He knows most people around here. He and his English wife, Victoria, have a small coffee bar. They mostly take coffee to the shop owners in the area, as it saves them having to leave the shop floor. And as you know by now, nothing can run in Greece without several morning coffees.'

She disappeared but was back in a few minutes. 'Yes, he does know someone who has a place but not sure it is still empty. He has gone to find out for you'.

Once again, Ruth and Bertie were impressed by the kindness of people, it was what you came to expect on Rhodes, but they never took it for granted. Five minutes later they were being led through the town and up towards the Knights' Palace.

The building was old but inside the first-floor apartment it was modern. Well, modernized some few years ago.

'Not sure if it is what I want, but it is certainly the best I have seen so far', he told the young woman showing them around.

'I will come up again later in the week, maybe Tuesday, and have another look', he said.

On the bus back to Lindos, Bertie chatted on about the pros and cons of the apartment.

'It is more spacious than anything we have seen so far', and Ruth agreed. 'But it has no redeeming features, like an old fireplace, or old doors. You could be in a modern apartment anywhere in the world', he argued on, mainly trying to convince himself that, regardless, it was a good find.

'But how much time will you spend in the house'? Ruth asked. 'The high patio gives you views as far as the medieval walls on one side and the Grand Master's Palace on the other. Surely the only time you would be in the house is when it is raining and when you are asleep'.

'You are right, I think I have been spoilt staying at Melenos. The tapestries, the comfy sofas, some of which we could recreate with a bit of imagination. The kitchen is wonderful, so many cupboards, a hob and oven, and we can easily get a microwave, a medieval one naturally. There is plenty of space to put it. And when my family and Claire come over to visit, they will want somewhere clean and modern to stay in. By the way, Claire has set her heart on getting married at Kalithea Spa. In about six weeks' time'.

Ruth said nothing. What was there to say!

If Bertie thought the cursory good night was a bit brief, then he put it down to tiredness. He had the apartment on his mind and the wedding. At first it hardly seemed to involve him organizing anything at all and now, suddenly, there was a list of 'to do's' from Claire, and the fact that her mother was coming over with her for two weeks before. He would take the apartment, but not on a long lease. At least one decision was made. He rang Ruth to tell her, but the phone was off.

Battery gone down again, he thought.

As Ruth unlocked the courtyard door a tear fell onto her hand. Another into the sink as she filled the kettle and the third onto the lid of the biscuit tin. The tea made, Ruth went into the sitting room and sank into the big leather armchair. Max's chairs, the ones he had shipped over from his home in England. Armchairs for them to share, to spend the evenings comfortably, here in Lindos, together. But he went away, far away, across a great divide and she sat alone.

What made Ruth think Bertie was serious, or in any way committed to a life with her? Why would he? No one else had been there for her, not her child's father all those years ago, and not dear Gerard regardless of the years they spent working and socializing together. And ultimately not even Max! An unfair and unreasonable thought, but true. Not long to live now and she would join her brother Francis, her dear mum, her dad, her daughter Ellen.

Another tear fell into the teacup. A big solitary tear, like the Greek rain before a storm. Only there was no thunder, no lightning lighting up the sky; no crashing of balcony chairs as they blew across the garden. Nothing only silence. And her quietly breaking heart.

****

HEATHER HAD EXPECTED that Tim and Trish would be back at the end of the holiday season, if only to collect their winter things and check on the house, but it had not happened.

Lord Rawlins had been down quite a few times when the American people were there, and he was calling in sometime during the next week just to check that they had left nothing behind them. Well, so he had said when he rang. But he also wanted to give Heather an envelope with a cash gift inside, just as a personal thank you for 'looking after' Henrietta and her friends. He did not know what arrangements had been made for the young Scots girl and her child, but he was sure that a little more cash in the kitty would not go astray.

As planned, Heather had brought Nigel back to Asklipios for a few days before he was to return to Canada. He wanted to check that there was nothing Heather needed fixing around the caravan, or the garden, before he left.

'It was such a blessing meeting you and Lucy. You have certainly been part of what I was able to achieve this year. Encouragement is a gift of the Spirit, and you made me feel so welcome. Just being here helped me prepare for the weeks in Prasonissi', he assured her.

The weather was still warm, but the next morning was dark and cloudy. Even a few drops of rain began to fall as Heather drove out of the gate. She was going to Kiotari to the supermarket to top up on milk and other bits.

Heather intended to have a special supper as it was Nigel's last evening. In the morning, she would drive him to the airport, regardless of his protest that, if he started early enough, he would manage on the bus.

'Too much depends on you getting that flight to Athens, so stop being so polite about it and just say thank you', she told him. So, he gave in graciously. When Bertie arrived, Nigel offered him a cold beer and they sat on a low stone wall chatting. Although overcast there was a slight breeze which made being outside quite comfortable. Bertie had never been to Canada, but it was on his 'bucket list', he said. 'There is so much to see, mountains, lakes, woods with wild bears and lovely little towns, like Banff for instance', Nigel told him. 'I will make some time free to show you around'.

'That is the type of introduction I enjoy. I am not much good at being an ordinary tourist. Unless you meet local people and get an insight into life in another country you might as well stay at home and read about it in a book.

E-mails were exchanged and they shook hands. 'Now that is definitely a date, not sure when, maybe when the weather improves after Easter, but I will be over, I promise you that'.

Heather was surprised to see Bertie there, but she had bought plenty of food, so their supper would easily stretch if he wished to stay. The kleftiko was freshly made from the restaurant, she had her own home-grown carrots in the freezer and only needed to add a potato each baked in the microwave. Even now, at this time of year, it would make the caravan too stuffy at night if she turned the oven on. With baklava from the village bakery and a tub of ice cream, all was organised. She would lay the table properly, outside, using the linen tablecloth bought from the Chinese shop. Even go very posh and use the matching linen napkins if it did not rain. And if it did rain do the same thing on the little table in the caravan.

Lucy jumped out as soon as her seat belt was undone and ran towards Nigel. He picked her up and swung her around as though she were made of feathers. He put her down again, steadying her for a moment in case he had made her dizzy, then she ran off after the kittens.

Bertie greeted Heather with a hug and a kiss on both cheeks, a bottle of wine and a bag of sweets for Lucy. 'I was thinking of staying over, I brought a bed roll with me, so I will not be making the house untidy', he told her. 'I have told Nigel I will drop him at the airport in the morning'.

Heather still had a problem calling the Hon. Bertrum Rawlins 'Bertie', but as he had insisted when visiting the house during the summer, then so she did. She invited him to join them for supper, which he accepted and decided that then would be an appropriate time to give her the thank you card with the gift inside it. He would drive Nigel to the airport in the morning.

Heather had started to unload the shopping from the boot. Nigel took the heavier bag from her and followed her to the mobile home. The sky had turned a blue black. She could not remember it getting this dark before, even in a winter storm. 'Thank you Nidge', she said, taking the bag from him, but he did not reply. He stood in the doorway listening.

'Don't forget you are eating with us tonight, as it is your last supper on Rhodes'. But he was not listening to her chatter, but to the strange rumbling noise that he had heard before, not in Canada but in Australia.

There had been three of them, John, Liam and himself. They had 'palled up' when sharing in a hostel in Sydney, then travelled via Aires Rock over to the west. They worked together on a banana farm in the middle of nowhere. Now only another week before they would go their separate ways. He to Canada, John to England

and Liam returning to Ireland as his mother was sick. They were sitting having a beer when the rumble started. Nigel wondered what it was. 'Sure, it is the water running down from the hills. It happens every year. Let's have a few dollars on it. Who can stay last in the river bed' They put a ten dollar note each under a stone and ran to the river bank. They slithered down to the dry riverbed and waited, but nothing happened. They started singing 'Wild Colonial Boy', as loud as they could, to drown out the roar of the water. But there was no water. Then it came, twenty foot high. John grabbed a tree overhanging the bank and held on for dear life. Nigel went with the water, managing to surface and take a breath, he was a strong swimmer. They found Liam's body two miles down-stream the next day.

'Lucy, where is Lucy?' He did not wait for a reply but leapt off the caravan steps and ran past the car to the empty riverbed. The little girl stood at the far side, the black kitten, the one that never scratched, in her arms. She saw Nigel and took a step towards him, the cat jumped, and Lucy turned to pick it up again. But she did not reach her pet before the wall of water overtook them both.

Nigel lunged forward, and stretching out grabbed something, he could not see what was in his hand. He hung on to the bundle that was Lucy as he desperately tried to get a foothold. He turned again, aware that he could not fight the power of the river and lifted the bundle above his head, grabbing at any items of debris with the other hand to keep afloat. They were travelling down towards the sea. He could do nothing but go with the flow of the thick brown water.

How much of this gritty mess he swallowed he had no idea. He coughed and choked and concentrated on keeping his precious cargo safe.

Then he saw it, a metal railing that had wedged against the pillar of the low bridge. He caught one end and jammed his body into the rails. They had stopped. His feet hit the gravel. For a moment he looked at Lucy's pale, mud streaked face. He held her tiny, limp body. He shook Lucy, and grasping her little trainers, held them higher than her once golden curls.

For most of his life Nigel had used words. Words of praise, words of thanksgiving, words of petition, sometimes biblical, sometimes his own inadequate words. Now there were no words as he put his fingers into the throat of his little friend, in a desperate effort to get a reaction from the doll like bundle of rags he held above the muddy water.

****

BERTIE HAD SEEN IT ALL as if in slow motion. He had watched Nigel run towards the riverbed. Then he saw Lucy and the rushing muddy water. He heard Heather scream as she too ran into the water. He saw her fall and go under. Within seconds she was a hundred yards down- stream, only her orange plastic jacket showing now and again.

He pressed his phone to call Panagiotis at the folk museum. Yes, Panagiotis would call the police. Yes, he could explain better, he could say exactly where the house and the riverbed were. It was done in a few seconds. The message was relayed. There was nothing else that Bertie could do. It was a long time since he had put his prayers into words outside the Sunday services of his Anglican faith. But without a second thought he was reciting The Lord's Prayer, 'Our Father, which art in heaven……..

Above the noise of the water, he heard the helicopter blades.

Only a parent would know why Heather went mindlessly into the fast-flowing water. There was no logic to her actions, no plan. It just had to be done. She had to be where Lucy was.

To Nigel's relief his instinctive first aid had worked, Lucy had coughed, and was sick. He held her tight and cried, his large frame shaking from the sobs. Everything had slowed down now, and his feet were firmly in the mud beneath him. The water level had dropped suddenly, and though it was still racing it was not something he could not handle. He could not guess how far they had travelled. He heard the sirens and saw flashing blue lights. There were people, a hand under his arm. He needed to let go of Lucy. They took her out of his arms, into the car and it sped away.

The police officer wrapped a plastic sheet around him. Was he o.k.? Did he need medical care? He shook his head. Much chatter in Greek. He sunk into the seat of a car and they moved off.

****

'How can a civilised country have a bus service that stops running from the main town at two thirty in the afternoon?', the passenger asked Mihalis as he got into his taxi along Mandraki harbour.

Normally any taxi driver would be delighted at the prospect of a straight run down the island, but Mihalis had the radio on in the cab and heard warnings of heavy rain later that evening. He would take the fare anyway he decided. He had a cousin in Asklipios and could stay there if the night was bad. No point in taking risks, leastways not where flooding was concerned. His cab was his bread and butter and he intended to look after it. It had been a good summer, especially with the American Henrietta over on the island again. He had taken them on lots of trips out, and although he did not like to accept, her friends had insisted on paying him well for the day. 'It's not a joy ride for you as you lose a day's work', they had told him, so he accepted graciously not only the payment for the taxi, but the leisurely lunch they insisted he take with them.

On the way back from dropping the passenger at his destination the sky turned a funny colour. The empty riverbed he had passed only half an hour ago was now a raging torrent, but it had not come over the bridge onto the road yet. He slowed down to look. It was not raining, so he stopped to get a closer view, and he needed a pee anyway.

He smiled as he added his contribution to the torrent below. He saw an orange bin bag. It was not a plastic bag but a coat. He made the sign of the cross three times as he went under the rail towards the water. He did not notice that the rain had started to fall in those large drops that always come first before a downpour.

Phil Davenport had been down to Kiotari to look at a car. He was disappointed, as the car offered for sale was in far worse condition than his own. It did not matter, he had enjoyed the bike ride, as it was not often that he got the opportunity to test his powerful motorbike on an empty open road.

The rain was quite refreshing after an overcast day, but he knew he needed to take care, as any grease on the road, mixed with a little water could be dangerous.

He saw the taxi parked on the bridge and his first thought was to wonder if the driver needed assistance. After so many years in the fire service it was an automatic reaction to assess any situation. He pulled up behind the taxi and could not see the driver at first. He parked the bike and ran over to the rail.

Mihali was leaning over into the water and pulling on an orange plastic bag. No, not a bag but a jacket!

One leap took Phil over the rail and down to where the older man was struggling to pull the jacket out of the water. No, not a jacket, a body. Phil slid into the muddy water and took the weight in his hands and then up onto his shoulder. Two steps further along the bank were outcrops of rock. He used those as steppingstones and with Mihalis steadying him, he was once more onto solid ground. Phil was kneeling on the ground using resuscitation techniques that had been part of his working life for so long that they were second nature to him. Mihalis called on the cab radio for help.

In the helicopter above was a young army pilot only recently posted to Rhodes. Now most of the tourists had gone home senior officers were taking the time to familiarise him with the area. A storm was on its way, so they would turn in a moment. Then they got the call to go to a bridge, on the main road near Asklipios. And they were almost overhead.

Despite Phil's efforts there seemed to be no response and it was with relief that he heard the helicopter. It circled, then landed just a few yards down on the road. Gratefully he handed Heather over to the experts with electronic shock and breathing equipment. He had done his best, and you learn to accept that ultimately, that is all anyone can do. Phil was not to know that whilst he had thirty-five years' experience in fire and rescue, this was the young pilot's first call out, and he was not even a medic. But beside him stood the first officer who was, and had almost as many years' working in these situations as Phil. Three minutes later the helicopter left with its precious cargo.

Mihali took Phil to his cousin's house. He would not stay long, just have a coffee and acknowledge Mihalis' vital part in the rescue. Then with handshakes all round he was on his way home. The rain had stopped again, but he knew to take care.

****

NIGEL HAD MADE a good recovery from his ordeal. He drank a glass of salt water, a remedy from his old hippy days in England, which never failed to make him throw up. They had searched Heather's caravan for her phone, then presumed she must have it with her. The next best thing was the laptop. It had a password on it. They tried the obvious, 'Rhodes', 'Asklipios', then 'Lucy', it needed numbers perhaps? She had been three in August, when was that? A birthday, at the beginning of August, when Henrietta was leaving. He would put them all in if he had to. 1813, 2813, 3813, it worked.

Email, thank God that was open, signed in all the time. Here it was, an email to her Dad. Was this the best they could do? Yes. They left an email with a message and the phone number.

Facebook? Her sisters would be on Facebook, they were, a private message. 'There has been an accident in Rhodes, please ring urgently. They left Bertie's number.

Panagiotis had rung to say the Air Ambulance had taken Heather directly to the hospital in Rhodes. Bertie agreed that there was nothing more either of them could do, and it would be pointless Nigel missing his flight back to Canada. Bertie would drive him to the airport as planned. He would be going up to the Old Town apartment anyway. Nigel put the kleftico in the microwave, and he and Bertie ate the supper with a few slices of bread, sharing the last can of beer. They sat on the caravan bench with a plate in their hand, not the way that Heather had in mind for what was to have been a special evening meal.

Why Ruth had not returned his calls for the past ten days Bertie had no idea. What had he said or done? Not agreeing over the apartment. What else could it be? Maybe she was busy with plans for the next craft group and just forgot to return the calls?

After all he himself had endured a busy week. He had rung the owner and accepted the lease, and on the Tuesday, he was in Rhodes to sign the forms. Then up again to get the electricity into his name, but he did not have a Greek tax number, so that was another office on another day. In the Forthnet office to get an internet connection he found that only O.T.E. put phone lines into the Old Town, yet another office, on another day! So, although he was a bit miffed by Ruth not returning his calls, he had no time to sit and think about it. He just presumed she was busy with trips up to the cemetery to help Christian, Ken and Tony keep the grounds tidy.

For all his laid-back way of life when he decided to do something, he went about it with enthusiasm and often an unnecessary degree of urgency. Anyway, he needed everything to be in order when Claire and her mother arrived in a few weeks' time. Driving down to see Heather he had intended to give himself a break whilst he still had the rented car. Now this awful thing had happened.

****

IT WAS TINA WHO realised that, as Ruth was not on Facebook, she might not have known about Heather. It was too important to talk about on the phone, so she knocked the spiti door just after ten the next morning. Although Tina had thought about how she would break the news, when Ruth opened the courtyard door, Tina dissolved into tears.

'Come in child and sit down. Nothing can be as bad as this. What can I get you, tea, coffee, water?'

'Nothing, thank you', Tina replied through the tears, and helped herself to the tissues Ruth had placed on the table.

'I was worried in case you did not know about Heather. There has been a terrible accident in the river, I thought you would want to know'.

Ruth shivered with the shock. 'No, I did not know, thank you for coming to see me. How awful; now, tell me slowly, exactly what has happened'.

'I don't know really it is all a bit muddled. Lucy and Heather fell in the river. Someone saved Lucy and she is in the hospital. Heather was washed further down the river, they found her, but no one seems to know if she is dead or alive'.

Tina started to cry again. 'I was thinking of that poor little girl with no mummy to look after her'.

Ruth was stunned by the story but she needed to be strong.

'I could do with a cup of tea please, so if you go and put the kettle on, I will make a few phone calls', she told Tina. It was an old way of dealing with a shocking situation, give everyone something to do.

Regardless of how she felt about Bertie, he was the obvious one to call. Some things are far more important than hurt pride, she told herself.

'Ruth darling, thank God you have rung, you were next on my contact list, though I am trying to keep the line clear for any calls from either the hospital or Scotland', he told her. 'I presume you have heard about Heather and Lucy? It was all so sudden'.

'You were there'?

'Yes, long story. I have rung the hospital, they say ring later as I am not the legal next of kin'.

'Oh, you poor thing, how awful for you. Where are you now'?

'I am at the apartment. Heather's parents will stay here when they arrive. At least we have sheets and towels. Josephine has been helping me, as she knows the places to go to, and the way to the tax office, but that is another story. When I have any news, I will phone you first'.

'Thank you, thank you', Ruth told him and closed the phone.

'Well, the best thing is no news is often good news', Ruth told Tina. 'There are digestives in the blue tin'. Tina fetched the tin out to the courtyard where they were sitting.

Any thoughts Ruth might have had about her relationship with Bertie had melted into the background. Like Tina, she was concerned for a three- year- old child who may have to grow up without her mother.

'I had better go now', said Tina, much calmer than when she had arrived. 'If I have any news I will ring', she promised. Ruth thanked Tina as she let her out the courtyard door.

What should she do now? Nothing. She sat down to finish her tea but could not hold on to her composure any longer. Now she was alone she cried. She cried for Heather, for Lucy and unashamedly, for herself.

****

KEN AND SHIRLEY WERE on holiday in Southport with their youngest daughter and her children. It was one of the grandchildren who told her mother she had a message. Karen did not quite understand at first. It was from Heather's Facebook page, but not from Heather. Karen rang the number given. If it is a joke, it is a poor joke she thought. The clear, clipped, very English voice left her in no doubt of the seriousness of the situation. He did not know all the details but a next of kin was needed as soon as possible.

Her mum and dad would need to go back to Dalkeith to get their passports.

'Calm down Shirl, sometimes these sort of phone calls are not as bad as it seems. There is no point in us both going. You stay here with Karen and the kids. That's the best plan'.

Ken had no idea what lay ahead during the next few days but knew that whatever it was he could cope better on his own. The journey back up to Edinburgh seemed to take ages. He tried to drive cautiously; it would not help if he were involved in a pile up. Eventually he was home and decided what he needed to sleep. He just crashed onto the sofa, exhausted.

Next morning Ken checked out flights and his neighbour drove him to the airport. He would get the shuttle down to Manchester and pick up a direct flight to Rhodes from there. He would not arrive till late Saturday night, but that was the best he could do.

All went well, he had an hour between flights. He slept sporadically during the second flight. Questions were spinning through his head; he tried to block them out. And Lucy? No information about Lucy! Why had they not used the phone? Heather's phone. Why send a message through Facebook? None of that mattered now. At last, on a journey that had seemed to last a lifetime, he saw lights twinkling below. Fasten seatbelts, they were landing. He only had hand luggage. It took a few minutes to get through the formalities and out into the warm evening air.

Phil was there, he put Ken's holdall onto the back seat and drove off.

'You'd never believe that the weather could change so quickly, like a spring day now', he ventured, not quite sure what to say.

'I grew up in the highlands. The one thing you can never trust is the weather', was the brief reply.

The hospital was sign posted. It only took them twenty minutes. 'You'll come in with me lad', Ken asked. Phil thought it a strange thing to say but was aware of the stress Ken was under. 'No problem, I'm with you all the way', he replied.

They drove round to park the car. 'This way', Phil said as he led the way in through the main doors. 'Bit of a maze like all hospitals, but I was here often enough to know my way around', he assured Ken.

They walked down a long corridor where one side was windows looking into a courtyard. They came to a lift. They had to wait whilst a man on a bed was wheeled out. Ken saw the sign for mortuary. He shivered and looked away. Tears filled his eyes, he gulped, trying to keep control.

Out of the lift and through a door, along and in another door. It said 'Intensive Care', maybe the doctors wanted to talk to him. He just wanted to get to see Heather. There was nothing to say that would make any difference. Not now.

'Good evening. Philipos', Doctor Kargolis greeted Phil with a handshake. 'And you sir, must be the father, you have had a long journey'. Again, he shook hands. He led them to an office. He offered coffee.

'It has been quite a battle, especially as we had to contend with a few broken bones. But she is a strong and healthy young woman, and I think the danger point has been passed'.

Ken looked at him and then at Phil. 'Pardon me doctor, I am Ken Mcfee. My daughter is Heather Naughton and I have flown from Scotland to identify her body after an accident'.

'No, no, your daughter is here, we nearly lost her during the night, and maybe we would not have had her at all if not for this young man. But we are over the worst now', the doctor assured him.

Ken put his head in his hands and let all the tension of the last hours rack his body.

'Lucy, where is Lucy', he asked through the tears.

It was Phil who answered.

'All tucked up in bed in Lindos by now I should think. Clare and Stavros collected her from the children's ward this evening'.

'Come with me now please', and the doctor led Ken through to the intensive care section. There were six beds but only one was occupied. Heather was sleeping, there were drips in her arm. Ken gently put out his hand and touched his child. She was warm and soft. To him she had never looked more beautiful than at that moment.

'You know lad that I was na' expecting to see her again, only to identify her. You immediately think the worst. The man I spoke to said she had been washed down a swollen river, what was I to think?'

'To be fair none of us knew the outcome, Bertie just wanted to alert you as soon as possible'.

'Och, dinnae think that I'm not grateful, just trying to work out what happened', Ken added quickly.

'No one knows that yet, it will take a day or two to put the pieces together', Phil told him.

'Lucy, I need to see Lucy'.

'Ken, Lucy is safe and well. The young mums all agreed she would be happier playing with the children she knew, as, apart from a cut on her arm, she is none the worse for her ordeal. In the morning they are having a special meeting of the 'Ladies and Little Ones' group, usually only held in the winter. That will be in Clare's place, the Atmosphere bar. They wanted Lucy to have her friends to play with tomorrow. Clare's two kiddies, Marietta and Nikos, and Zoe's three, Scarlet, Sony and Dara will be there. Once the message has gone out on face book, I have no doubt that the other young mums will join them. And all the toys will be out, which is just what a three- year- old needs. 'Keep her occupied', Zoe had said.

'So, with all due respect Ken, it is Heather who needs you, and to be there for her over the next few days as she recovers. Lucy is fine'.

'I am taking you to the Old Town now. A friend of Heather's, the man who contacted you, has an apartment there. He knows you are coming. It does not make sense to be down the island when you will want to go to the hospital in the morning', Phil told the still bewildered Ken. And Ken knew it was what he needed at that moment, someone to make sensible decisions for him. So much had gone through his head, the shock, the worry, the travelling, and now the relief.

In the darkness Ken had no idea he was passing over the medieval moat, through the Red Gate, and into the Old Town.

Phil handed his charge over to Bertie. As he got into the car, he checked his phone. A missed call from Chris. He rang home. 'Yes, sweet, just on my way home now. It is a long story, so don't wait up'. But he knew she would and looking forward to a cup of tea, or maybe something stronger, once again Phil Davenport drove off down the island to Kalathos.

And after two large measures of Glenfiddch, and a quick phone call to his wife, Ken Mcfee gratefully fell into bed and slept.

****

'GOOD MORNING DARLING, there is good news. Heather is on the mend. She is still in the I.C.U. as they don't need her bed, but there is no reason she could not be on an ordinary ward'.

'Good morning, Bertie. Wonderful news, thank you for letting me know. And how is Ken'?

'He is great, we went back up to the hospital at six this morning. He stayed with Heather until eight. Then we went to Auvergne for breakfast, came home to freshen up and I am going to take him to the hospital now. He asked how you were, I did not realize you had met him earlier in the summer'.

'Only briefly. Lovely man. So, no further complications?'

'Thankfully, none that I can see. Thank goodness it was not this week that Claire and her mother come over. I think that Leila is lovely, but I could cope with her as a mother-in-law'.

Ruth did not want to hear about Claire's mother, or anything else at that moment, but in the circumstances, she would not close the phone.

'The children have been calling Claire 'Mummy Claire', since they were told about the wedding, rather sweet I think.

'Sorry, can you repeat that? There is poor reception in the house, wait whilst I go outside', Ruth told him. There was nothing wrong with the telephone, it was in her head that the connections were not making sense.

'I said that since they have known that Claire and Marcus are getting married, they have decided to call Claire 'Mummy Claire', which is rather sweet, I think. Anyway, Ken is ready now, phone you when I have more news'.

There had been many times in her life when Ruth had referred to herself as 'a silly old biddy', but none where it would be more appropriately used than now. And what sort of person was she? To love and trust another in the most personal way and yet believe he would be planning to marry someone else! It was all too much of an emotional roller coaster. She needed to do some serious thinking. Or maybe that was the problem, too much serious thinking?

****

BERTIE FOUND IT quite a relief when an email from Claire cancelled the wedding plans. Well, not cancelling the wedding, but they would be getting married in Chilham; not Lindos.

Why was he relieved? Not a clue, but perhaps the thought of not having Leila, Claire's mother, at the apartment for about ten days, was part of his relief. He felt a bit mean, but he had offered. So he had done his best. Now he was off the hook.

He rang Melenos. It was embarrassing, as they had not taken a deposit. But the owner, Michalis whom Bertie spoke to, had been a friend for many years. They understood that if the bride's mother was unwell and not fit to travel, then it was circumstances quite beyond his control. They would contact the florist, and the town hall for the notary, and the photographer, someone that Bertie would have forgotten. Everything was unarranged as easily as it had been arranged a few months ago.

It did not matter that he now had every room equipped with bedding and towels. *You only buy them once*, he reasoned to himself, *and now they are there for any eventuality*.

The dilemma was that, because the date stayed the same, it fell the week of the school holidays. And Ruth had her craft group arriving for that half-term in October. And Bertie so wanted Ruth to be with him on this rare family occasion.

When he explained all this to Ruth over supper at Medeast, he was surprised by her reaction.

'Bertie dear, Naturally I would love to come with you. I was just waiting to be asked'.

'But we are together. Why would you not be asked?' He seemed quite puzzled that she would even raise the question.

'It is just that it would not interfere with your plans if the wedding was here on Rhodes, but a different story now everything has changed'. Ruth had to laugh. It was unusual to see Bertie looking dejected. He had this philosophy on life, 'if you can fix something fix it and if not forget it'.

'Well now, I am certainly not indispensable, in fact it will all fall into place quite easily. I would ask Peggy to do the admin, and the general meet and greet. After all, she knows everyone at the restaurants, and her own regular job would be finished at the end of the season. And don't forget, Tanya is coming to do the card making, and Margaret the Chinese painting as usual. Miles will be on hand I am sure, to assist Peggy if need be. In fact, come to think of it what would I be doing that week?' Ruth asked him with a laugh. 'But if I fly back on the Wednesday, I could do the silk painting'.

There were many times when Bertie had got the rather sharp end of Ruth's tongue, when she was trying to be serious, and he would not listen. But, on this occasion he was more than pleased to hear the 'voice of the teacher'. Organizing and planning, as Ruth had managed to do for most of her life.

Now all he had to do was check out the flights, not a difficult job with access to the internet.

****

PART 9

IF BERTIE THOUGHT he had a peaceful time ahead, not having the wedding to arrange, then he was mistaken.

He had walked down to Romeo's for a lunchtime snack, and was delighted to see Josephine there, having a coffee and chatting to George, the owner.

George stood to greet him, then turning to Josephine told her, 'Here is the man you need to speak to I am sure he will have all the answers, just let me know in good time what and when your transport is needed', he indicated the vacated chair to Bertie and walked away to speak to other guests.

Bertie sat as directed, and once armed with a beer and having ordered a variety of small Greek dishes for them to share, asked Josephine what the problem was.

'There is a film production company, coming from England in about ten days, to make a film on Symi. The whole project is crowd funded, which means the budget is minimal. The outstanding problem is the flight schedule. The plane lands late at night and the ferry is not until the next morning. George has offered to provide transport in from the airport, and even a meal for everyone the night they arrive. But they need overnight accommodation in Rhodes', she explained.

'And are they all arriving at one time', Bertie asked, thinking that he could ask Stergos for a discount on a block booking if there were more people than he could accommodate.

'No, fortunately it is staggered during the week, but the first group is the producer, his wife, two children, mother-in-law to mind the kids as his wife is an actress, and that is just the start. Added to that are a director and stage manager. An electrician and a lighting man are scheduled to arrive direct to Symi by ferry from Athens, as they will have a van with lighting bits. Other actors are arriving later in the week. Oh, forgot the make-up artist and Rebecca Grant's husband'.

'Rebecca Grant? Would you believe, Rebecca is my cousin. I have not set eyes on her since she was a teenager. Except to watch her in Casualty that is', he added, referring to her famous television role.

Josephine was at a loss for words. You get used to finding out that someone on a tour bus going around Monolithos lives next door to your granny, but this was such a strange coincidence.

'Yes, she never uses her 'top drawer' connections, but anyone doing a 'who do you think you are' would have a field day, except of course she knows who she is', he said with a knowing smile.

'Look, you know my town house almost better than I do. So, you plan it out, who is arriving and when. Then if you have too many bodies than beds, I will ask Stergos about his studios near St. Georges gate. He is bound to have vacancies now. Problem solved. Now I am sure you can manage some more salad and there is a cheese ball each' and concluded the conversation.

So, by the time they had finished their lunch, and Bertie had ordered another coffee for Josephine and a beer for himself, George came over to join them. And they were pleased to report that everything had been organised, just as he had predicted.

Bertie contacted Rebecca, so pleased that he was able to offer her and her friends somewhere to stay, even if it was only overnight. Unfortunately, they would miss each other, as the next week Bertie would be on his way to Chilham. Thankfully, there was bedding and towels. Everything they would need. And most importantly Josephine would organise it all.

****

IT WAS A MOTLY CREW that came striding through the gate of Diagoros Airport late that evening, smiling and giggling with nervous laughter, with relief. Their luggage and a quantity of lighting and sound equipment had arrived in Greece. The first part of the journey over.

Josephine held up a welcome card. No need, as all other passengers left the airport at least half an hour ago.

The CEO of 1066 productions, Chris Hastings, came towards her with a hug and a kiss. He introduced his wife, the actress Lorna Doyle, Lorna's mother, Anne, and the children, Seraphina and Daniel.

By the time Josephine met the director Navin Dev, production designer Chris Barber, sound recorder Lefteris Savva, and cinematographer Felix Schmilinsky, she gave up trying to remember who was going to do what in the production.

With Seraphina holding Josephine's hand, Anne pushing the pushchair, and everyone else managing luggage and equipment, they made their way to the three cars George and Heidi provided.

Twenty-five minutes later they drove over the moat, through gate at San Francisco, and arrived in the Old Town.

Everything was unloaded into the courtyard. Tarpaulins were hastily found to cover equipment, just in case it might rain, which it did not, but better safe than sorry.

A twin room was available at St. Georges studios. Navin and Felix suggested they would go there, as they could talk late into the evening, and begin plotting the scenes. Given the key and directions, they left. And yes, they would come straight back for supper.

Meanwhile Anne and Lorna gave the children some milk and biscuits and tucked them into their carry cot and sleeping bag, respectively.

By the time everyone chose a bed and dumped their belongings; the food from Romeos arrived.

Dishes and dishes of piping hot Greek food at its best. Beef stifado, lamb chops, dolmades, oven potatoes, and rice. With two bottles of red wine and another of sweet white, the scene was set. The evening air was warm, even at midnight. The atmosphere magical, relaxed, and chatty.

Josephine did not know that most of the people around the table that night had only met at the airport in London.

Not unusual for them, it was how the film and theatre industry worked.

Plates were emptied and refilled, certainly the guests were appreciative of the wonderful supper George and Heidi had provided.

The crockery was cleared; (Josephine stowed it away, so that no one would feel obliged to wash up. She would deal with that in the morning). Eventually at 2am, she tucked herself onto the settee in the small tv room, and with the alarm set for 6am, was soon asleep, as were the visitors.

Chris Barber, Production Designer (in charge of set and props) woke, showered, and started work before anyone surfaced.

He sat on the patio writing a prop journal for the movie. Chris has worked on fifteen feature films already including Casino Royale, Grey Hawk and Charlie and the Chocolate Factory.

(Of course, Josephine asked "What is Johnny Depp really like?" 'Yes', Chris replied, 'He is a nice guy!)

Although Chris had seen photographs of the locations, not having been to Symi made his and the director's task far more difficult. Thankfully, Terri Baker, a local Symi resident, had collected skeletal goats' heads and various other scary items.

Everyone gathered at the kitchen table, enjoying their 'full English' breakfast, except for Felix and Lefteris who were checking their equipment, bacon sarnie and a coffee in hand.

The transport, sent by George, arrived promptly at 7.30. two cars and a van.

The port was a scene of organised chaos, noise, cars, and lorries. Felix, most concerned about his cameras, spoke to the men at the dockside, explaining it was expensive goods.

To his surprise the answer came in a north of England accent.

'No problem, mate, we take stuff like this all the time. No worries.'

But, regardless of the assurances, no one relaxed until the equipment was loaded on to the ferry by the extremely kind and able staff.

Although Josephine had only met the group less than twelve hours ago, she was sad to see them go, but planned to visit Symi later in the week. She returned to the apartment, stripped the beds, putting the first load into the washing machine, and washed-up last night's supper dishes, ready to return them to Romeos. She made herself a coffee, lit a cigarette and went out to the patio. She rang Bertie, just to assure him all was going well.

****

Richard Syms arrived late the next day.

An actor since 1978, with a long list of appearances in television series such as London's Burning, Rumpole of the Bailey and Lovejoy and films such as The Iron Lady, Gangs of New York and, one of Josephine's favourite films, Truly, Madly, Deeply.

Although he arrived at almost midnight, he was certainly not ready to bunk down.

George knew that Josephine and Richard would be arriving at Romeo late that night. Despite the hour, George invited them to Romeo for a welcoming drink and chat. A takeaway had been prepared and after a glass of wine, Richard Syms, world renowned actor, and Josephine, Savaidis coach escort, walked back up a deserted Socrates Street. Over their late supper Josephine and Richard had a long and interesting talk and shared a bottle of Retsina.

I am an Anglican vicar, now retired', he explained. 'Over many years I managed to combine my service to God and film and T.V. work'.

Regardless of the late night, Richard was up before seven, and after a quick cup of coffee, walked down to Korona harbour.

****

Once again, the apartment was ready for the next guest, and this time Josephine could not resist putting a post on Face Book. The response was as expected. Many of her friends and their friends envied her the task of meeting Emmerdale actor Kurtis Stacey, when he flew into Rhodes to make his first film.

Backpack unceremoniously dumped into the bedroom, a quick shower, and Kurtis was ready to explore the Old Town.

He was amazed by it all, the Knight's Palace, the high walls, the towers, and the Pink Mosque. His first thought was to find a souvenir shop to buy gifts for his mother and Nan. That done they took a leisurely stroll back along Mandraki, stopping for a drink at the Top Three.

That evening Josephine took Kurtis to Romeo and introduced him to George who had invited them to dinner.

Romeo was as usual buzzing with customers, a Turkish celebration and the live music giving the place a party atmosphere; They ordered a Greek plate for two, (which was far too much), and packed with more Greek specialities than they could eat.

Kurtis commented that his friends and family would be surprised he was trying the Greek plate, as he is not too adventurous with food, but he now had the photographs to prove it. After a great dinner, topped off with chocolate and cheesecake it was time to go home for the weary traveller rest.

Next morning Josephine and Kurtis walked to the taxi station on Mandraki, as his ferry was leaving from Arcadia Harbour.

Kurtis was given an open invitation by Josephine to come and stay in her own Lindos home, bringing his mum and nan as well, if he wished.

****

So much was going on that Josephine almost forgot that her own mother was arriving next day, fortunately at the same time as Rebecca Grant and her husband Ivan Pierson. So, Heidi drove the family 4x4 to collect them.

The first to arrive were Josephine's mother on a flight from Birmingham, and Zoe Wilson, the make-up artist, coming in from Manchester. After the initial greetings and introduction, they were ensconced in the café, whilst awaiting the arrival of Rebecca and her husband.

But half an hour after the plane from Heathrow landed, there was still no sign of Rebecca and Ivan. The arrivals area had cleared, and they were nowhere to be seen. They could not get lost between Gatwick and Rhodes. But where were they?

Zoe rang Rebecca and … yes, they were in Rhodes airport, but Rebecca's luggage had disappeared.

Not the best start to a week of filming. Unfortunately, Rebecca's case contained more than just holiday wear. She had brought an antique dress, once belonging to her great-grandmother, Lady Ernestine Bowes-Lyon, which she planned to wear in the film.

She was upset, but her husband and friend Zoe, were with her.

Zoe and Rebecca worked together often. On Symi, Zoe would do the special effects make-up and Rebecca was to play the part of Stauroula. They chatted on the drive back, as did Josephine's mother and Heidi, who had met several times over the years.

'Oh! my goodness', Rebecca exclaimed, when they entered the walled city. 'Bertie told me it was a very special place, but I did not expect anything like this'. Minutes later the guests had been shown to their rooms. At least there was room for everyone as Josephine again camped in the small tv lounge.

'George and Heidi have invited us down to Romeo restaurant here in the Old Town', Josephine told them all when enjoying an early evening glass of wine on the patio. 'Perhaps if we leave in about half an hour', she suggested, and it was a welcome distraction from thinking about the missing suitcase and whether it would ever appear.

On the way to the restaurant there were frequent stops for photos, particularly outside spectacular places like the Suleiman Mosque.

Romeo was full, with live music and dancing; it was the ongoing Turkish celebration.

George welcomed his guests with his usual charm and found their reserved table. Before Josephine's mother had sat down, Andreas who had left his 'meeting and greeting' spot outside, had grabbed her for a spot of Greek dancing. This was great fun, and she loved the fact that she was welcomed and indeed, remembered.

Greek salads and huge slices of bread arrived, together with drinks and Zoe, Rebecca and Ivan tucked in. The film crew who had come days earlier had sent text and raved about the feast that would await them at Romeo!

The three travellers had forgotten that there was still a main course to come…., then to their surprise, the expansive Greek plate arrived with an assortment of traditional food (fantastic for new visitors, as some may not have tried Greek food before). They tried everything, moussaka, dolmades, cheese balls and much more and time rolled on, whilst the musicians continued to play, and guests were up dancing traditional dances around the tables.

Eventually, and rather regrettably, they decided to call it a day, and a night. There would be an early start in the morning. George, the most generous of hosts, was thanked, with handshakes and goodbyes. A great night at Romeo, and a perfect introduction to Rhodes. A leisurely wander home through the deserted streets of the Old Town and into bed.

After a 'tea and toast' breakfast, (no one could manage anything more), they all walked down to Korona harbour.

****

Josephine and her mother travelled over to the island with Rebecca, Ivan and Zoe. On arrival on Symi, while the others went straight up to meet their fellow cast and crew members, Josephine stopped to say hello to their old friend Takis at the leather shop. They sat nearby having a coffee. 'Has it been a good season?' she asked him.

'Very good, better than last year. Plenty of German and Scandinavians, less from England.

The pound against the euro has changed, makes a big difference', he replied. 'Call in on the way back, if you have time, I have something for you', and Takis was back into his shop as another customer wandered in.

After lunch Terri Baker took them to the deserted village film set.

It was a flurry of activity; equipment coming up from below, make up being applied, young extras arriving dressed in black as instructed (with logos on their tee shirts? Oh no!)

Extras being roped in to carry yet more equipment, more extras enrolled from the village residents who had only come up the hillside to watch the filming.

Rhiannon Wheeler, a Symi resident and make-up artist, was rushing to make up everyone involved, and even some that were not involved, just in case they were needed.

Director Navin Dev was here, there, and everywhere. He struck the classic pose which you always see in movie making documentaries as he stood and formed a frame with his hands to envision the scene. The next minute he was perched on crates at the top of the steps surveying the location and the hive of activity (or maybe just taking a moment to himself!) Then he was instructing a group of school lads, preparing them for their big scene.

Another problem. A generator made too much noise and echoed around the almost deserted village. Thankfully, not every house was empty, and kind residents allowed equipment to be plugged into their home supply.

Neil Gosling, who had been photographing the project from the beginning, had already helped with the equipment. He was then asked to take a part in the film. When Josephine and her mother left, he was being covered in black make up, ready for the burning scene!

What an interesting day. Knowing the people concerned, the camera man and the director, the leading actors and their families, it seemed they were part of that magical world of film and theatre.

Just as they came to Takis' shop he called out to them. 'You have time to catch the ferry', he said, glancing at his watch. 'Come in, come in', and they went in between the rails of beautiful leather coats and hats. 'I had one strange job a few weeks ago. To make two leather waistcoats and sew a panel into the back. The pattern on the back said Rhinestone Cowboy, whatever that means. The panel came over in a package with special buttons. Looked like pearls in the middle and sparkle bits on the edge. Very fancy. In the evening light the gems looked almost real. They were for two English men, into American dancing it seems, there were shirts as well.

'Wow, I hope they paid well', Josephine asked her friend.

'That was another funny thing, they did not pay. It was a cash transaction into my bank from Athens. 'Here, I have some of the fancy stuff left over, it's no good to me. Put it on those birthday cards you make. Send me one for October the 24th, just to remind me not to take on such a crazy project again'. Josephine put the small bag into her pocket, and with a wave, they rushed to board the ferry.

****

Five days later the filming of The Judas Curse, (later called the 13th) was finished, though there would be a huge amount to do in the UK before the movie would be ready for release.

The visitors were leaving Symi and passing through Rhodes on the way home. Josephine waved goodbye at the port.

Except for Rodrigo, the lighting gaffer, who had come to Symi via Athens, had a plane to Madrid the following day. At supper time it was off to Romeo Restaurant once again. Rodrigo, a charming young Spaniard, (who would not have looked out of place in a Knights and Maidens classic movie), had worked on short films and commercials in various countries and it was a fascinating evening, discussing the filming of The Judas Curse, the technical side of the project and his part in it. The terrain on Symi had made the work physically strenuous. It seemed to have been a real community effort, with many locals lending a hand wherever they could and having small parts in the movie. It was getting late by the time she and Rodrigo had finished chatting, over yet another splendid meal at Romeo. He thanked George for his hospitality. Rodrigo would be flying to Madrid early the next day.

****

Now the laundry needed to go into the washing machine so that everything was 'ship shape and Bristol fashion' for Bertie's return. That done, Josephine made herself a coffee, and taking her cigarettes, went out onto the patio. Her mother was already there, browsing through a writers' magazine. They smiled. No need to say anything. Another 'Greek moment' had passed successfully. Would the last film crew member to leave Rhodes Island, please turn out the light?

PART 10

HRITASHA BRAHMA AND HER boyfriend, Kyle Morris, sat on the steps of the patio high above the small back street in the Old Town. They were waiting for their friends to arrive. It was not exactly a party, but more of a reunion, as most of the young people, all at university in Athens, had spent last summer working for the Waterhoppers diving school on Rhodes.

If the League of Nations needed a junior section, they could do worse than recruit from these young friends, drawn from many corners of the earth. This year, Hritasha, from Kolkata, India, on her third summer with the diving school, and studying Applied Psychology in Athens, had met up with Kyle, her South African born boyfriend, and they hoped they might be working together some of the time.

Also, at university in Athens was another friend, Emanuel, proud of his Slovakian gypsy background, both he and Kyle were on course for degrees in Maritime Archaeology.

Mario Bordonada was the exception, as he completed his four- year degree in Occupational Therapy, had spent last summer diving in Thailand, and looked forward to starting his first therapist post in the autumn. Mario was from Spain. But, this summer, where better than working for the diving school on Rhodes.

And this amazing group of young people, and many others, were on hand to instruct and guide the diving school clients in perfect English. Not English with a Liverpudlian twang, or a Brummie mumble, but clear, precise, beautifully enunciated Oxford English. It also meant that between them there was hardly a modern European language that was not spoken and understood. What better aid to health and safety could there be?

****

Carol had booked the day out for Richie, as from Rhodes Town. She had not seen much of the medieval city during her last stay and thought they could drive up together. She would look at the architecture and the shops whilst he was out on the boat. They would meet up later, go to

Romeo's for a leisurely meal, then drive back down the island.

Hritasha greeted Richie on his first morning at the diving school, a boat moored in Mandraki harbour.

She explained the dangers of diving, and completed a detailed medical questionnaire, which they both signed.

'And you have never dived before?' she asked.

'Well, yes I have. I am an experienced Metropolitan police diver in England', he replied. 'In fact, I train divers', he added.

'But did you give say this when you booked?'

'No, my wife did the booking as a gift. I have never told her that I dive. She worries about everything to do with my job, so it is often kinder to say nothing'. Richie did not see what the problem was. Different if he had said that he could dive when he did not.

'You see, you could have had an interesting day out with the experienced divers on the wreck. But the minibus has gone now. Would you just like to cancel today, and we book you for tomorrow's trip? I am sure you would enjoy that better. You see, this is a beginner's instruction class'.

Richie laughed. 'Look, where I normally dive is in muddy London canals, looking for unpleasant things. It will be a pleasure to dive today, wherever, and even if it is a basic class, you can always learn something'.

The matter was settled and before long they were leaving Mandraki harbour for Kolymbia.

Up on deck, Richie found himself sitting next to an Australian man of a similar age. Nick introduced himself.

'I am over from Sydney, though I am Greek, born on Symi. My sisters thought I would enjoy a day diving. They booked me in as an early birthday gift. Told the guy on the phone I was an experienced diver. Well, I guess I am, if you count diving off the cliffs on the Whitsunday Islands. Then I have done Cairns and the barrier reef, but no need to dive there, you see just as much when snorkelling, or just swimming under water with a pair of goggles. But, as I have never done a PADI course, I am having to start at the beginning today.'.

'It all sounds good', Richie told Nick. It was not often that he revealed his police connections, but, hey this chap was from Australia, so he wanted to return the compliment of an open conversation. 'I dive for the police, in London. But today should be a welcome change, clear water, and not to find something you don't want to see'. They both laughed.

'Fancy a beer?' asked Nick. 'That is if we are allowed one before diving'. He went off to find out, and Richie relaxed and took in the beautiful coastal scenery.

At the bar Nick met Simon. Nick invited him to join Richie and himself on the deck. 'He's an English guy, working with the police. Something to do with refugees he said. Bit of a pensioner's party today I think, we are all past middle age', Nick laughed, as he led the way back up to the deck.

By the time the boat reached Kolymbia, all three men had been given basic safety instructions. Nick was quite intense, not wanting to say something foolish in front of his new mates. Richie concentrated as well. He was finding the whole process interesting, not having listened to another person instructing for many years. He considered the safety aspect extremely well done, and even thought that they should take a new look at the manual when he got home, in case any relevant points were taken for granted, just because they were for police officers. He steered the subject away from his police connections. Simon was quite nervous if the truth were known. But he was enjoying the 'craic' with the lads, and that helped keep his fears away.

Richie was now diving for the fun of it. He had the opportunity to look around, see the rocks and vegetation, and the colourful little fishes swimming in and out of the crevices. Marine life was not something he had considered when on a fishing trip.

When not actually in the water, the three men chatted amicably. They considered a day out on the wreck to be the next step and would enquire before they left the boat. Simon said he would give that a miss, as it would be his last day on

Rhodes. He would not leave Geoff on his own again.

The trip to the wreck was organized for two days ahead, and Nikos and his sisters were invited to join Richie and Carol at Romeo's later that evening.

Simon, he declined the offer. 'It has been a long day, and thanks guys for the company. Lee has offered me a lift back to Pylona, so it would be crazy not to accept'.

They agreed to meet up again next year, and with handshakes all round, Simon left the company. He had enjoyed it once he felt confident in the water.

Must be great to go out onto a wreck, never know what you might find in those places, oh well, maybe next year.

Over supper at Romeos the Australian Greeks (or should it be Greek Australians) Nick and his sisters, Vicki and Pandy, talked about their childhood. Born on Symi they had relatives who lived in Rhodes Old Town and were often travelling back and forth in their father's old fishing boat.

It was a lovely evening as everyone got on well and joined in the chatter. Carol was surprised to learn that Vicki ran her own 'Home Care' company, and naturally they enjoyed comparing the different procedures, and basically 'talking shop'.

Nick told Richie about a friend he had met on face book.

'When we met up for a coffee, the guy asked me if I knew who he was. So, I told him only the name he used on face book, John Kalliosis. He went on to explain that he was the guy who organised a breakout from the main jail, using a helicopter. It had failed, and John had done time for his part in the job. The funny thing was that John, and the pilot became good friends. After all, the pilot only had a slight flesh wound to his leg, but the compensation was massive. It set him up for life'. The men continued to chat whilst the ladies tucked into their cherry pie and ice cream desert.

'He wrote a best- selling book about it', Nick told Richie, thinking as he was in that line of business he might be interested in the story. 'It is called 'We Dared', definitely worth a read', Nick added.

It was time to call the evening to a close. The girls exchanged e mails before saying good night.

For Carol and Richie, the drive back down to Lindos did not seem that long. They left the car in the square and walked hand in hand down to Villa Koki. The moon shone clearly on the water, the sunbeds were all lined up like soldiers.

******

Two days later Nick was down at the harbour in good time for the minibus trip down the island. It had been agreed to pick Richie up at the Kalimera Café at Lindos reception.

Neither of the men had explored further than Lindos and welcomed the bus trip as much as looking forward to their diving experience on the wreck.

They went carefully through the safety instructions again and were kitted out in wet suits and breathing apparatus. The visibility was not as good as in Kolymbia, but they were down deeper, and other people were on the wreck, which made some disturbance.

It was Nick who spotted the shirt first, the arms caught tight onto a jagged piece of metal. He signalled to Richie.

Richie had put his Swiss army knife into his boot as he donned the wet suit that morning. Now he pulled it out and opening the blade, cut the collar and cuffs from the rest of the material. Even at that depth the embellishment had a shine. He handed the cuffs to Nick, with an appropriate signal, and a 'thumbs up'. It was time to return to the surface.

Everyone admired the souvenirs as the bus travelled back up the island. Just a modern piece of jetsam, not treasure to be handed in for assessment.

When Nick showed his find to Vicki and Pandy they were delighted. Once back in Sydney they would have the little bits of costume jewellery made into bracelets. Richie kept the collar for himself. He would hand it in, 'found it on the beach sir', he would tell them. And with a bit of luck the rest of the shirt would be there next year when he and Carol came on a proper holiday. Well, that was the plan.

LEE O'FLYNN ALWAYS arranged a day out, diving on the wreck, for his staff at the end of the season, though some had left the previous week to go back to university or start their career.

The day started well. What a joy! A clear blue sea with no other divers to disturb the water. And more importantly, no responsibility for someone else's life. It was not something that was constantly on their mind when working. They followed safety procedures to the letter and thankfully, clients were sensible and followed instructions. But to be diving for the fun of it was different. Yet if you asked these young people why they would shrug their shoulders and smile. They were educated young adults and took responsibility in their stride.

But that morning the gang had been in good spirits, laughing and joking, recounting some of the daft remarks that tourists had made to them over the past few weeks. Once at the wreck they donned wet suits and apparatus ready to dive.

It was Hritasha who had spotted the shirt first. Soon other friends were examining what was hanging on a spike under the hull. Kyle decided to unhook it and take it with them. On the minibus going back up the island they gave it a more careful examination.

'I think it might have some value, but I am not sure,' Kyle had suggested. He was from South Africa and gems were a constant source of discussion at home. 'Then what about you keeping it, to investigate' David told him. Kyle looked at Hratasha, as it was her discovery.

She agreed immediately. 'But we are all in this together', she told them, 'and Emanuel and Mario, we should not leave them out'. So, it was arranged. The next morning Kyle had rung his father to ask whom he should go to in Greece. A week later he took the items to Katsidonis, a small jewellery shop in a street near Mandraki. He had then emailed the good news to everyone involved. Yes, it would take some time for the gems to be sold on, and too early to even estimate the value properly, but it ran into a few thousand euros each. How exciting.

****

PART 11

THE FLIGHT TO STANSTEAD was uneventful. A girl from the airport assistance team was waiting for them with a wheelchair. Although they were the last to leave the plane, the way they whisked through passport control made up for the delay.

Not Gatwick but a damn site better than Manchester,

'Where is your shirt', Geoff had asked Simon earlier that morning. 'Oh, safe enough', he had replied.

'Not in your suitcase is it'?

'No, it is not. Stop making a fuss, it is only a bloody shirt. What's wrong with you'?

Geoff was tempted to say more but best not. Just as well, for at that moment Simon had no idea where it was, only that it was somewhere in the Mediterranean.

He would not have given the shirt to Miles if it had meant so much to the old man.

How was he to know! After all it is only a bloody cowboy shirt, not the crown jewels, he reasoned.

With a few Bacardi and cokes the flight had been quite enjoyable. Geoff was great company when in a good mood, and the holiday seemed to have done him a lot of good.

Simon wished he had taken more care of the shirt, shame to upset the old boy now.

'Put your shirt on before we go through the customs bit', Geoff whispered. 'There is a toilet over there. I am alright here with this girl. The luggage won't be around yet'.

'I don't have the shirt, I lent it to Miles on the boat to Haraki and did not get it back in time'.

'Yer what', was all Geoff managed to say before he started to cough, and then choke, his face went red, and he was holding his chest and having a job to breathe.

'Mr. Morris, Mr. Morris, tell me, have you any pain', the girl from assistance yelled at him. But he just held his chest and was gasping for breath.

'Emergency, emergency, suspected heart attack, carousel number 3'. She had hardly spoken the words before two paramedics were on the scene. Geoff was lowered unceremoniously to the floor. They gave one tug at his shirt and the buttons flew in every direction.

'My shirt, my buttons', he managed to whisper in between the coughing fits.

In that one frenzied moment, it dawned on Simon what all the fuss about the shirt was for. The buttons, glued on and not sewn, were what Geoff had bought back from Symi. This was the debt he had gone to collect. This was the pay-off for God knows what. And now it was scattered on the airport floor.

But the people leaving the flights were mostly Brits on their way back from an amazing holiday. No way would they take anything from a sick man and his friend, not even a few glass buttons. One lady, Lauren, was holding three that her children Sophia and Luc had picked up. Seeing this, other people looked around and handed her a few more. Eight in total, she passed them all to her husband Jamie and he passed them to Simon. Even if they had known the value of the bits of glass they had in their hands, they would have done the same thing.

Geoff was quiet now. He had an oxygen mask and they had placed him on a stretcher. Other medics had arrived.

'Got your cases mate? O.k. let me give you a hand. The ambulance is outside. Your father sir? Oh, just a friend is he sir. Follow me now', and Simon with the pearl and diamond buttons in his pocket was led outside.

He got in the ambulance, and it sped away.

Geoff Marsham died before reaching the hospital.

And all over a bloody cowboy shirt, and a few quid, Simon thought.

Just a friend, he had told the medic, but Geoff was the only father he had ever known.

What happened next became a bit of a muddle for Simon.

Thank God Geoff got back to England before kicking the bucket was his immediate thought. The paramedics explained that there would have to be a post- mortem, mainly to establish that they had done their job correctly.

'Then he will be taken to a local funeral parlour, and your funeral director will come and collect your friend from there. Of course, arrangements need to be confirmed by his family'.

There were no family, just Simon and the girls. And Pete the egg man.

'All this will take time, so may I suggest you go home now and let his family know what has happened'.

Simon, with both lots of luggage piled onto a trolley, took the man's advice, and got into a taxi. It was dark now, and he nether knew nor cared which motorway he was on or how near to Folkestone he was.

The house seemed strangely quiet as he put the key in the front door. He rarely came into an empty house.

Simon had already sent the couple, booked in for that week, along the road to the Polish people. He would do the same for Alan and Pam, who were coming at the weekend. Trying to be in holiday mood for visitors was the last thing on his mind.

He decided not to ring his daughters till the morning. He knew Pete, the egg man would want to know, but tomorrow was another day.

Thankfully, there was half a bottle of malt in his lounge bar. He took it upstairs with him, not bothering to get a glass.

He did cry; first time since his wife had left.

'Only a friend', he had told the medic.

But Geoff had been more of a father to him than many an ordinary Dad.

****

SIMON HAD ASSUMED that Geoff was from London, but when he rang the solicitor, the first name on Geoff's list of 'emergence numbers', he found out otherwise.

Geoff's ancestors were from the small village of Chilham, near Canterbury. There was a grave, and Geoff had listed his wish for a service in the parish church, cremation, then his ashes interred in the family grave. The cremation would be a private affair, as any mourners were to go to the Woolpack for lunch, then transport back to London for those who needed it. The solicitor even had a list of phone numbers, friends Geoff had specifically asked to be notified. The first job was to go and register the death.

'Stay where you are. I will come and collect you', Robert told him.

Simon was feeling worse that morning than on previous days. The wave of despondency clear as he spoke on the phone. The enormity of the situation was beginning to sink in.

Ten minutes later they were waiting to be seen, and within half an hour Simon was inviting Robert into the Fisherman's Rest. 'Thanks, but no thanks, I have appointments later today, so am off home for a sandwich. You know where I am if you need me. As I said, the best people to contact are Sullivan and Sons in Dover. Nothing is ever too much trouble for them. And you speak to the owners, which makes it all easier. Particularly with the special requests.'

Simon rang his daughters that night. He did not say anything about the circumstances. 'Just a heart attack, can happen to anyone past a certain age, and your uncle Geoff was well on the way to eighty', he had told them.

Simon had already showered and shaved when Pete arrived, so he looked better than he felt. He went through the rigmarole of explaining what happened.

'He had these fancy shirts made, on another island, and we went over and picked them up. We were having a great holiday, stayed in some nice places. Then, when we got to Stanstead, he asked me where my shirt was, the fancy one with the Rhinestone Cowboy on the back. In the end I had to tell him I had not got it'.

Pete could wait no longer. 'Well then who has?'.

'Hold on a minute. What do you know about the cowboy gear? What is going on here?'

Pete was thinking on his feet, well not on his feet as he was sitting down.

'Don't get upset, this is a difficult time'. The look Simon gave him was enough for Pete to know he had to come clean, well almost clean.

'Geoff told me he was owed a few quid by this guy in Greece. He went over to bring back some stones, stuck to the shirts. Enough for him to get what he was owed, and a bit of bonus. The rocks were pretty hot, as I understand it'.

'So, he chokes himself over a few lousy green backs. We have enough here, from the guests. I don't understand'.

'It's a way of life, you get bored without some job on the go'.

Simon put the fish and chips which Pete had brought, into the microwave.

End of conversation? Well, enough for today, but he knew there was more to the story than that. And why had he told Pete about it and not him?

But Simon new that none of that mattered now, it won't bring him back.

****

THE THING ABOUT Sullivan and Sons Funeral Service was that it did not look foreboding. The office was on the corner of the High Street in Dover. The building was painted white, and welcoming. Well, as welcoming as it could be for people who did not want to be going there in the first place. But it is the last thing he can do for his friend, so Simon wants to do everything right.

Paul came towards him and shook hands.

'Good morning, Mr. Goodman, I am Paul Sullivan. I am pleased you were able to come to the office. It is much better than talking on the phone. Though we would have been pleased to visit you at home if that is what you preferred. Take a seat'.

Paul asked about the circumstances, listening as Simon explained the whole story. Often people needed to express their grief, perhaps say things they could not say to family members.

'I know the distances are a problem, but it has got to be the traditional black horse drawn carriage. Geoff spent most of his life in London. His friends, those that have not passed on already, would think it a poor 'do' if it were not traditional'.

'Tell me exactly what you wish for the day. How it happens is our responsibility. Nothing is too much trouble, nor cannot be achieved. It is difficult to talk about money, but every step of the way we will clearly explain the costs involved'.

'No problem, Geoff had his own finances, and even if he had not, that would still not be a problem. But thanks for mentioning it, must be a difficult time for some people'.

Paul smiled sadly and nodded, thinking about the previous clients that morning, but he said nothing. What was there to say. He continued.

'In that case, if you agree, with details of Mr. Marsham's bank we can send our invoice directly to them. It is the only creditor the bank can pay from his account'.

'Yes, not a problem, and what is done is done. Geoff would like to manage his own affairs.

The men let a smile pass between them, to acknowledge they understood the reference to the tenacity of Geoff Marsham.

Simon continued. 'Only one more thing, I did ask about the 'country and western' shirt, which he was wearing when he was taken ill. But I have had second thoughts, and have brought you his best suit, and his good shoes, and shirt. I did not know what was needed'.

'That is fine. The car is on the way to Essex at this moment. We will bring everything back.

'I think I have most things, as the hospital gave me his wallet and passport. But thank you. Something else I need not think about'.

They stood and shook hands. Simon did not know what he had expected, but it was not as difficult as he thought. Decisions had been made. But he was not going to tell Pete the truth, not yet anyway.

****

Pete had a lift organised to drop him in Folkestone the next day. Simon met him in the Fisherman's Rest.

'Well, would you like me to get the western items passed on, you don't want these geezers knocking on the door'.

'Don't I?' Simon asked, disliking the way the conversation was going.

'Only trying to help'. Pete was not sure how much to say. He had known Simon all these years. Geoff was gone. Will he lose Simon as well? He hoped not, good friends were few and far between.

'Well, if you change your mind, give me a ring'.

'No need, not about the shirts. One is at the bottom of the sea, and the other Geoff is being buried in. That takes care of everything'.

Pete the egg man coughed and spluttered his last mouthful of coffee across the bar floor. He was trying to draw breath, and Simon was thumping him across the shoulders. At last Pete cleared his lungs and gave an inward gasp. Simon put a Bacardi into his hand, he sipped from the glass.

'Jeez, that is all I need, I will be up for manslaughter if another old git kicks the bucket in my company'. Simon was trying to make light of the situation, but truth was, he was shaking.

'That shirt is worth close on half a million. And I thought you said it was a cremation anyway? They are not going to put all that bling into the system'.

'Oh, but they are, it was my special request'.

Pete the egg man looked totally drained.

Simon continued. 'I was at Sullivan's yesterday and everything has been arranged, with a horse drawn carriage as well'.

Simon was beginning to feel sorry for Pete. After all, the deal he had going with Geoff might have killed him, but to be fair, Geoff could have died any time, in a hospital bed in Folkestone. At least he had a bit of adventure those last few weeks.

Simon handed a Tesco plastic bag to Pete.

'What's this, I done my shopping yesterday,' he said as he looked in the bag.

'Bloody hell son, you did not say you had this,' he gasped, as he took Geoff's waistcoat out of the tissue it was folded into.

'It is Geoff's. You are about the same size, and he would want you to have it. There is quite a bit of bling on the back, may be a bit O.T.T. for every day.' Simon was playing down the gems, pretending to have no interest in them at all.

'This is like gold dust. Do you have one yourself?' he asked.

'I did, but could be at the bottom of the sea, same as the shirt, no problem. What is gone is gone'.

Pete was near to tears. This would get him off the hook. Not that the guys he was working with would turn funny or anything, but if you take something on as big as this has been, you do feel responsible. A lot is hanging on seeing it through.

Though he did recon he could knock a few stones off the back, just to keep him in beer for a few more years, and to see Simon O.K. Fair was fair.

The waistcoat was back in the Tesco bag, and Pete's lift back to Margate had arrived. There was no date set for the funeral yet, but they would probably meet up before then.

****

Simon began to think about his own situation, now everything was organized. He and Geoff never talked about 'what if', and he did not know how he stood regarding the house, and the business.

The solicitor said Geoff's will would be read after the funeral. But whatever it said, Simon had enough savings to buy a small place back in Devon, that would be one option. Or rent the house in Greece, yes, a nice little B and B in the sun.

It was the first positive thought since Geoff had died, and it made him realise that life had to go on. Just the funeral, then he would have plenty of time to consider what to do next.

******

WITH HIS CONNECTIONS throughout the county and beyond, it was not difficult for Paul Sullivan to arrange Geoff Marsham's funeral exactly as his client wished. There were three cars leaving Folkestone. One for Simon and his daughters, who had arrived home by train the evening before. They would meet up with the funeral carriage near Chilham and follow the hearse.

The second for the Polish couple who ran the guest house nearby, and Mabel and Doug, from the newsagents. The third was for the landlord and two mates from the Fisherman's Rest.

A car would collect Pete from Margate and his lorry driver friend, so he had extra help getting in and out of the car. They would bring an ordinary wheelchair with them.

From London there were two coaches, and quite a few cars. Quite a good turnout for an old chap who had no family.

All were assembled outside the old parish church as the beautiful carriage, drawn by two black horses, came slowly down the lane. Everything was as Geoff would have wanted. The horses wore black feather plumes and their coats and harness shone in the autumn sunlight. The carriage was glass, with black and gold fittings. Two workmen stopped and waited for the funeral procession to pass by, removing their caps as a token of respect.

The service was short and to the point, Abide with me and The Old Rugged Cross. The vicar thanked everyone for travelling so far to bring Geoff home to rest and reminded them that the cremation would be a private affair. Lunch is provided in the Woolpack, and he looked forward to meeting them there.

The organ played, and Simon and the girls led the way, following the coffin out of the church. It was placed into the carriage again, and once everyone was assembled, the carriage moved off on Geoff Marsham's last journey.

****

PART 12

FOR RUTH AND BERTIE the flight to England was easily arranged, as most of the tour companies were still operating. Ruth suggested they go to her home in Stowe first, so that she could pick up an outfit she thought would be suitable for an autumn wedding.

With his usual 'got a problem fix it' attitude, Bertie thought it far easier to just buy a new suit, or whatever it was she wanted. He had no idea that any woman of a certain age much prefers a tried and tested ensemble, dress, coat, shoes, gloves, and handbag. They compromised. He went to his friend near the airport to pick up his car, whilst Ruth had her reliable taxi driver to take her to Stowe.

Ruth was not as relaxed as she usual. She had a certain anxiety about the situation between her and Bertie. When you have been brought up to have a certain code of moral behaviour, it is difficult to shrug off your misgivings and live outside that code. Now she was going to meet Bertie's family. But how will they see her? Just his 'bit on the side', or will they not even think to question their private arrangements. In today's society does anyone even think about these things. But she is not of this new generation.

Somehow it seemed to be different when in fairyland, a Greek island, with sun and sea, and young people, and the not so young, with new ideas about what is acceptable, or not!

Ruth was up early next morning and went to Mass, but not to the church in the village. She did not want to be greeted by her former community, with many good wishes, and their joy at seeing her unexpectedly amongst them. Instead, she drove to Buckingham. The priest at the altar was Indian. Not much unusual about that these days, but what was unusual was his Irish accent. The service was quiet and peaceful. At these morning weekday services, most of the congregation were elderly.

The brief sermon was about prayer.

'There was a man with a problem about his health, and being a good Christian, he took the problem to the Lord in prayer. After several weeks without any resolution, he decided to stop praying. In his dreams a voice told him 'Go up the mountain and push big the rock, go push it every day'.

So, convinced he had a mission to make the road safe from the rock, he went every day and pushed. Eventually he came back to the Lord in prayer. He said he had pushed for many weeks, and nothing had changed. He could not move the large stone.

A voice replied. 'I did not ask you to move it, that is my job. I only asked you to push. Now look at how strong and healthy you are, going to the mountain every day'.

After the service, Father Jason introduced himself, explaining that he was a Carmelite friar, originally from Kerola, but now based in Moate, Ireland.

Ruth did not stay for coffee. She had come that morning with a prayer, and now she had the answer. Stop worrying and everything will work out. No, she would not give up on her prayers.

****

Ruth and Bertie met two days later, at a service station on the A 34 and before long joined the traffic on the M25. Lunch was at another service station along the M 2, and they arrived in Chilham in the late afternoon.

Ruth had not told Bertie that she had looked up Chilham village on google last week and had been pleasantly surprised by the beautiful setting of the Grange. In all the years she had spent living in Canterbury, with her brother and her daughter Ellen, she had never been to Chilham. Now, via the internet she had explored the lovely church of St. Mary's, and was surprised to find that Chilham was in the Doomsday book. She hoped that she would have the chance to wander around the old church buildings before Claire's wedding.

Claire was up in London, so it was Marcus who greeted them. The children were still at school, he explained. Ruth's first impression of Marcus was all positive. He had given Bertie a hug but greeted Ruth with a very English handshake. This always seemed quite strange when you were used to the enthusiastic kiss on both cheeks from people in Greece. He took Ruth's case, and they went directly to Bertie's apartment. Ruth tried not to stop and stare at the grandeur of the stairway, the high ceilings of the rooms, and the beauty of the old furniture. Even the windows were stained glass. Once inside the apartment there was a small serviceable kitchenette area. On the opposite side one door opened to a large lounge, with massive sofas and a bar in the far corner. The other door held the bathroom and two bedrooms. Marcus put her case into the smaller room, and Bertie winked at her surreptitiously. She frowned back at him, then smiled.

'Tea as soon as you wish, I will be downstairs in the office, not really doing anything now, just tidying up', Marcus told them.

'Well, this will do us for a few days. Hope you find it comfortable. There are a lot of stairs I am afraid, so you learn very quickly not to forget anything when going out'.

'It is beautiful my darling. I never imagined it would be so old. What an amazing place'.

'Yes, it still seems strange that I inherited it. As I have told you, as a child I only came here in the holidays, a sort of companion to play with my cousin. We were the poorer branch of the family', he added, making the mime of playing a violin for sympathy.

'Let's go down for tea, I really am gasping', was Ruth's response. 'Unpacking can wait till later', and they went off to find Marcus, and his promise of a brew.

****

Next morning after Bertie had cooked a 'full English', as the Lindos cafes call it, they put on raincoats and taking umbrellas, walked into the village.

Even in the rain Ruth could see how beautiful everything was. Thatched cottages, lovely English gardens, the larger Georgian houses with the black and white exterior, and presiding over it all, the parish church.

Bertie pointed out that some low thatched buildings, standing back from the road, were the village halls. 'The reception will be in there on Saturday. They are going up to London tomorrow and having a Jewish ceremony in the synagogue near where Claire's mother lives. Then on

Saturday there is a blessing here, in the church, which will have all the paraphernalia of bridesmaids and best man, with the reception in the large hall. Then everyone goes home and turns out for an evening 'do' in the Woolpack, our local pub'.

'It all sounds exciting, but exhausting', Ruth told him with a laugh. 'Do you think we will last through till the evening?'

'Oh, it is quite easy, when you start to flag, you have a whiskey or two, and start all over again'. Ruth gave Bertie an exaggerated frown. 'I think one whiskey might be enough for me, with ice. Can you get ice with a drink here?' then Bertie realised she was just teasing him by pretending not to know, and he leant over to kiss her, and the umbrellas clashed. Which led to more laughter.

They had now walked down to the church, and through the gate. A shiver went through Ruth, as she recalled the last time she and Bertie were together in an Anglican parish church. Max's funeral. But she said nothing as she did not want to spoil the moment with sadness. She was unaware that Bertie was thinking the same thing, and in a way, was regretting bringing Ruth into the old stone building.

But, once inside it was nothing like the little church in Ripple. Yes, the walls were stone, but everywhere was open and wide, and the ceilings high. They did not go exploring around but found a pew about halfway down the main isle. Bertie stood back to allow Ruth into the seat. He followed and went onto his knees and put his head into his hands in prayer. Ruth also knelt, she made the sign of the cross, and with her hands clasped in front of her, began the Hail Mary under her breath. She then offered a prayer for Marcus and Claire, that their future may be happy and fulfilled. She made the sign of the cross, then sat back onto the pew.

She had been unaware that Bertie was already seated. She smiled at him, and he reached for her hand. It was so quiet, so beautifully quiet.

'Ruth', he hesitated. 'I was thinking it would be such a good idea if we got married. What do you think?' and without waiting for a reply asked, 'Ruth, darling, will you marry me'? She did not reply but nodded her head and smiled even though a tear was escaping down her cheek.

'It won't be that bad', he told her laughing, 'No need to cry about it'.

'Not even a tear of joy', she asked. 'No, not even that', was his reply as he put his arm around her and kissed her hair.

He dug into his jacket pocket and produced a thin silver ring with a small pearl in the diamond setting. He put it onto her finger, and it fitted because he had measured a ring she wore but had left on the bathroom shelf one morning. It was Max's engagement ring. And he wanted Ruth to be able to wear them both, hence the slim fittings of his ring.

'I think that is how it should be worn, we both want to remember Max', he told her. Then they sat in silence for a few moments, recalling memories of their friend.

When they left the church, it had stopped raining. They considered going into the Woolpack but agreed they were in no mood for company and took the long road back to the Grange. On the way, they passed the cottages that had belonged to the small farm the wine makers had bought. Ruth said how pretty they looked, and that it was a shame they were sitting empty. It was the reaction that Bertie hoped for, but he said nothing. Looking at them could be left for another day.

They had dinner that evening with Marcus and the children. Later Marcus was driving up to London to join Claire and her family. The children informed them that they only had one more day at school, and yes, they could get themselves up and ready for school, and their friend's dad collect them. It was all arranged.

****

THERE WAS ONE PLACE that Ruth wanted to visit with Bertie before returning to Rhodes. There, near the grave of her beloved daughter, Ruth would tell him about Ellen.

They drove into Canterbury, and first Ruth took Bertie into St. Thomas of Canterbury Catholic church, which was only a short walk from the Cathedral. The church was dedicated St. Thomas a Becket, a bishop murdered in his own cathedral in the Middle Ages.

Bertie had to admit that in all his years of living in the area he had never been inside before. There were far more statues and paintings than in the Chilham parish church. But also, it was smaller, and with relics and side chapels, it seemed a busy place. Ruth lit candles; three, one for Ellen and Francis, one for her parents, and the last one for Bertie and herself.

They did not stop longer, as too many tourists around. Also, she wished to drive out to the cemetery. Bertie presumed that her brother was buried there, and he was, but the flowers Ruth carried were for Ellen. Bertie read the inscription on the stone. A child, and only eight years old, how sad, how very sad. A relative? Perhaps Francis' child? He did not ask.

After laying the flowers Ruth led him to a bench over by the wall. There was still some warmth in the autumn sun. They sat quietly for a few moments, and then, when she felt able, Ruth told him about Ellen.

'It all seems so long ago now, and yet, in a strange way, it could be yesterday. I had just finished my degree at Cambridge and during the last year at Uni, I had fallen in love with a boy from Ireland. I expect it was having the same background drew us together. Naturally, all those years ago, it was not the usual thing to sleep with your boyfriend, but we did. And I assumed that once our finals were over, we would plan our life together. But I assumed too much, and he arrived at the conferring ceremony with his fiancé. And I was pregnant'.

Ruth waited a moment before continuing. Bertie had reached for her hand, and they just sat in the tranquillity of the afternoon.

'That September Francis was starting his degree here in Canterbury. I told my parents that I would look for a temporary job in the area, and to help my brother financially, we would share a flat.

So that is what happened. Francis was not intending to marry, he felt sure of that, so the arrangement suited us both. We never told anyone that we were married, never told anyone we were brother and sister. People just assumed what they wished. But for Ellen, Francis was the only daddy she had ever known.

For many years we lived just like an ordinary family. Then our darling child was diagnosed with a tumour. It was the most heart-breaking year for all of us. We watched as our little one slipped away. After Ellen left us, Francis went to friends in Carcassonne, where he could lead his life how he wished. We had bought the apartment, and Francis returned to Canterbury about three years later. By then Father had died, and I went home to be with mother in Stowe. And that is what has shaped my life until going to Rhodes and meeting Max.

So now you know who I really am, apart from being a rather old-fashioned retired teacher'. She smiled at him, that sad smile that sometimes engulfed her. Now he knew why.

There was silence except for the birds singing, just little sparrows chirping away to each other. It was beginning to get cold, after all, it was October. Ruth walked back to the grave, put her hand gently on the tombstone, just for a second or two, then they returned to the car.

****

CLAIRE MADE A STUNNINGLY beautiful bride, her jet-black hair piled into an open pleat, under a pill box hat with sparkling short veil. Her suit was cream brocade, with a three-quarter length pencil slim skirt. A silk tangerine blouse complemented her tan shoes. She did not carry flowers but had a corsage of pale orange roses on her wrist. The wedding was everything one would expect, though it was a blessing. Claire and Marcus had married in a synagogue in north London a few days earlier. Beside Claire, as she entered the church together, was a tall and handsome groom, dressed in an immaculate morning suit, with a waistcoat and cravat that themed with the bride's outfit. As they came to the altar rail, they were joined by the children. Next to the groom now stood his young son, who was best man and next to the bride was a little flower girl, his daughter. The vicar made the blessing ceremony light and yet romantic. He included the children in his brief address, telling them to take care of Claire, as she was not used to being a mummy, and would need their help. And that their daddy also needed help now he was getting older, to the amusement of the congregation. Certainly, a day to remember for everyone.

After the photos, they went to the village hall for their reception. For Ruth it was quite strange to be a guest at the top table, part of an extended family. Strange but delightful. Only when she began to look around the room, did she notice how many of the original craft group were there.

Mel and Keith, naturally, Rob, with his wife Beth, Margaret with her daughter Judith. Tanya was on the next table. Margaret and Tanya were staying overnight at Gatwick and flying to Rhodes the next day.

There were no formal speeches, at the request of the happy couple, so Bertie was surprised when Marcus stood, and gained the attention of everyone by tapping his glass.

'Thank you all for coming, and just to remind you that the afternoon will continue with a tea dance once the tables are cleared. Then this evening, we will meet again in the Woolpack, to which you are all invited'. He stopped to take a sip from his glass. 'Now, yesterday I was told something and was sworn to secrecy. But I had my fingers crossed behind my back, and as you know, it does not count if you do that'.

There were claps and laughter, and a few calls of 'get on with it'. 'Well, yesterday, a little bird told me that my dear uncle, the Honourable Bertrum

Rawlins and his lovely lady Ruth, are now engaged to be married'.

There was an outburst of clapping, and hoots of joy. Also, shouts of 'not before time' and 'you kept that quiet', and a few other teasing remarks directed at Bertie. And the inevitable call of 'speech, speech'.

Bertie stood and simply said. 'It is my pleasure to introduce you all to Ruth, who has kindly consented to be my wife'. He took Ruth's hand and asked her to stand. Everyone clapped. Ruth smiled and then they sat down.

Staff appeared from nowhere and moved tables, with the help of the gentlemen guests. It took only a few moments to restructure the room. When the keyboard and violin started to play, the craft group came to speak to Ruth, and admire her ring. They asked about Heather and Lucy, and they were assured that they were making a good recovery. Ruth thought that Beth was pregnant, and whilst the others chattered on, she tactfully asked Rob. Yes, he was thrilled to say she was, a most unexpected, but joyful surprise for the couple. Once everyone from the group had managed to have a few words with

Bertie, they left the reception, promising to meet again in the new year. Unlike most of the other guests, they had to face a long drive home.

After one or two sedate waltzes, made so enjoyable by the fact that in these circumstances Bertie became an acceptable ballroom dancer, the band changed to folk music. Sir Roger de Coverley, the Gay Gordons, and others which most guests remembered from their school days. Back to traditional ballroom to end the afternoon.

At six o'clock the band stopped playing and everyone realised it was time to go home. Well, that was until they regrouped at eight, for the evening session in the Woolpack.

It had all been organised so that no one had to think about anything. Cards and gifts would be packed away and later delivered up to the Grange. Nothing was a problem.

****

ON THE SUNDAY morning Claire, Marcus and the children went off to Disneyland Paris. They were a family now, and that was how Claire wanted it to be. 'So, as a family we are going to Paris on honeymoon', she had told Marcus when he asked her where she would like to go after the wedding. Bertie and Ruth now had the Grange all to themselves. They went to church for the Matins service, as it was the third Sunday in the month. Then into the Woolpack for lunch. Pierre was there, so they were able to thank him, on Marcus' behalf, for the gift of champagne, but he was flying back to France that evening, and still had things to do, so would not join them for lunch.

It was a crisp and sunny day, so they strolled down lanes that bordered the Grange, well some of it, and along footpaths that crossed the fields. Ruth was surprised when they turned down a small lane and came out near the cottages again.

'I suggest we renovate and make them our own', Bertie said, after they had gone inside and had a good look around. 'I have enjoyed having the apartment, but, as I explained, I have no sentimental attachment to the place. When we are staying here, I would much prefer our own space. Ruth was unsure. 'But what about Claire's plans for the university courses? Will she not need these houses as well, eventually?'

'I doubt it, as it was assumed that the winery people wished to include the buildings in the sale. Also, they need a fair bit of modernising, and that would cost money. I would suggest buying them anyway, so they would not lose any income'.

It was certainly a tempting idea, to have their own house here so near Canterbury. Ruth loved everything about the cottages, which, knocked through into one some years before, had a spacious living area. And yet, there was a certain feel to the rooms, an English version of the spiti may be? a memory of her grandmother's cottage in Ireland? Something she could not define, but for Ruth it seemed perfect.

They did not have time for further discussion as Ruth was returning to London on the four o'clock train. She had things to do in Stowe and was flying back to Rhodes on Wednesday.

It was a bit strange saying goodbye. In these few days, everything had changed for them. They now had a future to plan. And big decisions to make about where they would call home. But for Ruth, silk painting with the craft group was her priority, and in many ways, she was looking forward to returning to Lindos.

****

SELLING THE HOUSE IN Stowe had been a hard decision, but once made Ruth found herself quite relieved. After all, she would soon have a home in her beloved county of Kent and be near to her brother Francis and her daughter Ellen. For Ruth, there was something immoral about having two homes, not even counting the spiti in Greece. The estate agent who visited had given her an amazing price, much more than she expected. He suggested they put it up for ten thousand above that, but let it be known a quick sale was needed and be prepared to accept less than the asking price, to the right buyer, with cash to exchange. Ruth had watched lots of T.V. programmes about selling property but had no experience. So, she told the estate agent to do whatever he considered appropriate.

She handed him a set of keys, as she would be returning to Rhodes on Wednesday. Almost organised and her bags packed, Ruth phoned Merle and invite her for a drive to Towcester.

They could browse the shops, have lunch, and talk about the wedding plans.

'It will be a very quiet event, just a few old friends and Bertie's family. Fr. Paul is driving down from Milton Keynes, so is happy to collect you on the way. No date set yet but sometime before Christmas'. They parted company with a hug and looked forward to meeting again soon.

Now Ruth had a spare day to check through the items she needed to take from the house. There were times when making lists made life easier, and this was certainly one of them. There had already been two people to view, but no commitment. Then, a young couple, originally from Sligo, with two children, and a third on the way, knocked her door.

They ended up all sitting in the kitchen, and over tea and digestives, Ruth was only too pleased to tell them she would accept twenty thousand below the asking price, even though they had not mentioned any bargaining. Also, except for the items with a red sticker on them, they could have the furniture. There were also sheets and pillowcases, and a lawn mower in the shed, which might need a bit of oil on it.

Ruth knew her parents would be overjoyed that another young immigrant family would live in their house. In many ways she felt it had all been planned by the One Above, and she was so excited for the couple that the emotional wrench of leaving her family home almost slipped away.

PART 13

WHEN RUTH HAD THOUGHT about moving the autumn craft week to half term, she guessed that some of the guests might be teachers. She was wrong, all of them were.

This did not bother Peggy, after all she had been teaching I.T. before most people understood what I.T. meant. Add to that many years in Lindos with her own restaurant, Sinatras, she was no amateur at dealing with the public. The icing on the cake, (looking down the list Ruth had left for her), everyone was arriving with a friend, colleague, relative, whoever! So, hopefully they would enjoy the sessions, then go off for lunch, the beach or both, and arrive back for the afternoon slot.

The Sunday brunch had gone down well, Broccolinos had made such a great job earlier in the year, that Ruth had rebooked immediately. Peggy had told the group about the Sunday evening barbeque on the beach at Skala, but did not think she need organize them, or book a table at this time of year. Meals were booked for the rest of the week, starting with Medeast on Monday, and ending at Nefelli on Friday. Wednesday would be the free day, and she suggested a minibus to Symi Island, well, a minibus to the ferry to Symi island, if enough people were interested, followed by time to take a brief look around the Old Town, and supper in Romeo. Everyone thought this a great excursion, and she rang Pete Moore for availability and costs. Another item sorted.

Tanya had arrived bringing all she needed for her first card making sessions, then raid Ruth's craft boxes for the rest of the week, if needed. Margaret had already assembled her tool kit of rice paper, brushes, and ink on her usual table in the shade. Ruth would be back from England on Wednesday evening, joining the group in Romeo's if her flight landed on time, and start teaching the silk painting on Thursday. With everything so organized, from the craft lessons to the meals and excursion, Peggy did wonder how she would occupy herself all week.

On Wednesday evening Ruth arrived on Rhodes and joined the guests at Romeos. She would be teaching silk painting in the morning, so travelled with the group to Lindos.

Ruth thought everything had worked out right. As it was really Peggy and Tanya's event it seemed appropriate that she should leave them to preside on the final evening. She would join the group for supper at Nefeli.

And that concluded a very enjoyable craft week for both guests and tutors. None of it could have happened without Peggy and Ruth proposed a toast to thank her. Most of the guests had already exchanged contact details. They had jelled so well as a group that they planned to take the same holiday the following year, if Peggy agreed. And with a glance of acknowledgement to Ruth, it was all settled

****

ON SATURDAY MORNING Ruth met Margaret by the tree at the 404 bar and they walked together to the square. Jenny was on the way to the Beer and Bier and stopped to tell Ruth that the grandchildren from Athens were arriving for half term. Captain Takis was sitting on the bench. He waved and blew Ruth a kiss. She and Margaret took the long road down to the big beach. They waved 'hello' to Rocos as he hosed down the floors at Oasis. Rosanna and Nikos were at Palestra, relaxing now that their son Thomas, his English as fluent as his Greek and Italian, was organising everything. At Nefeli the Hawaiian sunshades were looking exotic. Marianna had now inherited the restaurant from her father Nicolas, but she was busy and did not see them. They walked along the wet sand, past the Dolphin, with a morning wave from Mihalis and Enrico.

Across the goat path to the small beach and they reached their destination.

'Wait a moment', Ruth said to Margaret. They walked on a few steps and there, outside the bar where the men sat and played cards was the blue wooden chair. On the back in white was painted the letters 'Socrates'. Ruth and Margaret did not need to say anything.

As they turned to go up the path Ruth made the sign of the cross, 'yia mas Socs', she whispered under her breath, as she retraced the few steps to Giorgos 2.

Tina was waiting at one of the little outside tables. Holly, over from England, was coming along the beach towards them.

Once they were seated Jacob came to take their order.

'Good morning, ladies, what can I get you on this lovely morning'? As though he did not know it would be croissants and coffee as always. There was a shattering of crockery from the kitchen, 'Oh something has broken', he needlessly told them. Margaret looked at Ruth before she started to sing.

'Morning has broken like the first morning,

Blackbird has spoken like the first bird',

Ruth smiled and thought Margaret could not have picked a more appropriate tune, and to Tina's embarrassment Ruth and Holly joined in singing,

'Praise for the singing, praise for the morning, praise for them springing, fresh from the Word'.

They started to laugh as both realised 'sweet the rain's new fall', was hardly appropriate, but undeterred Margaret continued.

'Mine is the sunlight, mine is the morning',

Oh! The many times Ruth had played this tune in school assembly!

'Praise with elation, God's recreation of the new day'

'Tina raised her eyebrows and shrugged her shoulders. 'English', she said to Jacob. He nodded in agreement and went to fetch their coffee.

Yes, Ruth did miss Lindos, and wished she had taken a few more days. But her flight was booked for that evening.

****

PART 14

RUTH DID NOT WAKE until after nine o'clock.

At first, she felt quite disorientated, and it took a moment to realise she was in the apartment at the Grange. She stretched lazily and opened her eyes to find Bertie standing with a tray.

'Good morning sleepy head', he teased her. 'Would Madam prefer to take tea in bed'.

'I would not move from here even if the roof fell in', she told him.

'Oh! Now was that a yes or a no, I presume a yes, in which case I will put the tray down and sit by the window until madam is ready to be served'.

Finally, Ruth was awake, but she had no intention of moving. Then the thought of a mug of tea and a digestive took priority and she opened her eyes again and sat up.

She sipped the brew slowly, it was hot and weak, just how she liked tea.

'I know leaving Stowe was quite sad for you, with memories of your family and your childhood',

Bertie said gently. 'But now you have made that decision we can go ahead with plans for here. We can of course stay in the apartment for as long as we wish, take our time in sorting out the cottages'.

'Yes, but let's make something to aim for', Ruth suggested. 'Shall we say in our own home before the wedding? Is that reasonable do you think?'

Bertie laughed. 'If you say it will happen, it will happen my love. But not if we sit here drinking tea all morning'.

Ruth remembered that she and Claire were going into Canterbury. She hastily showered and dressed.

It was the first time Ruth and Claire had been into town together, and it was to be such an enjoyable day out. Once the car was parked, both agreed on a coffee stop first before any shopping. It was some years since Ruth had spent time in the Canterbury shopping precincts and was surprised how different it looked. There was so much choice, and they went from the department store into the fashion shops, 'just looking' they reminded each other. But by the end of the afternoon Claire had a new winter coat and Ruth a long velvet skirt, M and S of course.

Next thing was to find a small café and an indulgent cream tea. The first 'cream teas' sign they saw was outside the library, and they were not disappointed by their choice. Real thick clotted cream which you do not find on Rhodes.

Claire suggested she fetch the car, as it had started to rain. But Ruth was quite happy to walk back to the car park, after all they could only get wet.

It had been a lovely afternoon, one which Ruth hoped would often be repeated once she was back living in Kent. On the drive home, they chatted about how Claire and Marcus had enjoyed their trip to Paris, the children, the farm, the new venture into residential courses. In no time at all they were back at the Grange.

Bertie had also driven into Canterbury that afternoon. He had decided to treat himself to new shoes, quite a rare quest as when you buy shoes from Loakes they last such a long time.

Then he was going around the corner to the Butter Market to meet with Bob Thompson, an old RAF colleague. He had invited Bob to be his best man, no date set yet, but some time before Christmas. They had a sandwich and a beer together. Missions accomplished; he drove back to the Grange.

****

PART 15

IN CHILHAM, BERTIE left the Grange first, driving Marcus and the children, into Canterbury.

It was a chauffeur driven classic BMW that arrived at the door of the cottage to collect Merle, Claire and of course, Ruth. A fine white knitted top, that once belonged to her grandmother, complemented the velvet skirt, and matching royal blue court shoes. Her only flowers were cream roses attached to a clutch bag. Elegant and timeless.

To Bertie's surprise there were quite a few friends, also in dress uniform, already seated at the back of the church. He looked at Bob, and by the grin on his friend's face, knew he had organised their attendance.

He walked across to where Pete was parked, in the side aisle on his scooter, and they shook hands. Bertie was pleased his old friend had managed to get into Canterbury for the occasion. How near they had come to a sticky end with the diamond business! Both men agreed it would be their last venture, regardless of the good causes they had supported over the years. Only they knew what drove two decorated ex-servicemen to risk so much.

Ruth had no idea that Margaret, Tanya, Miles, and Peggy knew the time and date of the wedding. She was delighted to see them, and Steve from Steps bar as well. Marcus took her arm.

It was an ordinary midday mass except that, to the surprise of the small congregation, there was a wedding ceremony first. Father Paul was on the altar, concelebrating with Canon Anthony Charlton, the parish priest. It was quiet and dignified, just as they had planned.

Outside the church photos were taken. It was the only thing that Bertie had asked for, a professional photographer. He had also booked a studio session, for an official portrait, but not today.

It was hardly lunch time, but as everyone had taken an early breakfast, it did not seem to matter. They walked along to the restaurant where they sat in the lounge, pre-lunch drinks in hand, chatting about everything and nothing.

Bertie held Ruth's hand. He just did not want to let her from his side. This had been a long time coming, meeting someone to love again, getting married. Such a long time.

He could not imagine her looking lovelier. Even if they had met years ago, when they were young and a little foolish, he doubted he could have loved her more than he did now. He refused to let 'what if' enter his head. They were married, and for as long as God allowed, that was how it would be. Ruth turned and saw the rather wistful look on his face. She smiled, and gave his hand a gentle squeeze, and a look that said she understood.

It was late afternoon when they said goodbye to their guests, wishing them a safe journey home. They drove back to the cottage. But now it was quiet, and as Lord and Lady Rawlins sat in the dusk, in the new conservatory, glass of wine in hand not a word was spoken.

The car engine disturbed them. Marcus shouted across 'Childcare all organised. You did not expect to get away quite so lightly, did you?'

Ruth and Bertie looked at each other.

'Your guests are waiting at the Woolpack. Champaign is on ice. Get in, get in', he commanded, indicating the car door.

And the rest of the evening was spent in convivial company, accepting their congratulations and good wishes.

>   Tomorrow will be another day.

****

AND THEN

When back home in Canada, Nigel Lawrence never told anyone about Lucy. But it is a small world, and a couple from Calgary were on a cruise ship, docked in Mandraki. When walking in the Old Town they picked up the free English newspaper. It carried an account of the rescue, and named Nigel Lawrence, the Canadian who saved the child. They often attended the same Pentecostal church.

Heather and Lucy spent the winter at home in Dalkeith, but Lucy never really settled. When enrolled in nursery school, she constantly asked for her little friends from Lindos, and could not understand why she did not see them. Although it seemed ungrateful to her parents, to be honest Heather was also missing Rhodes. She mentioned this in an email to Ruth. Ruth told her that only Tina was staying at the spiti, perhaps she might like to go over for a month or two, see how she felt about being there.

Heather told Tina of her plans, and Tina was delighted that Heather and little Lucy would be coming to stay. She hoped it would be their forever home. It would be great company, as the days dragged a bit until she started work in April at the Crazy Moon bar for the summer. Her friend, Sara, had married Peter, and happily settled in Bournemouth. Heather was also pleased to have Tina's company. Ruth assured them both that when she and Bertie were in Lindos they would stay at Melenos.

Mel and Keith had travelled to Ireland several times to stay with Neil and Edwin, even helping with big Dublin weddings or large high-class venues, and all enjoying the company so much. Their daughter Carol had not married her boyfriend but moved back home before the baby was born. Safe with her loving Mum and Dad.

Carol and Richie had a small lottery win. They decided to retire. They moved to Italy, to a town called Bergamo. Naturally, Richie's Italian is now fluent, and Carol understands most things. They could not be happier. It was only a short flight to Rhodes, and they travelled to the Old Town each year to meet up with Nick, Vicki and Pandy. Nick and Richie went diving on the wreck. There was no sign of the shirt with the glitter on.

'It was probably worthless anyway', Richie told Nick.

It was over dinner at Romeo that night Vicki handed Carol a bracelet in a satin lined black box. 'We had it all valued' she told Carol. 'I got cufflinks; Nick added, flicking his wrist for all to see. You girls got a bracelet. Probably worth about twenty thousand Aussie dollars each. Handy enough for a few hours work', he laughed. 'Here Richie, your cufflinks', he announced as he handed over another black box.

Pete the egg man has been unwell and did not make it to Malta this last winter. He misses meeting up with Simon and Geoff. Bertie has driven over to Margate to visit him on several occasions. They manage to laugh about their near miss with the law. Never again.

Simon has sold the Folkestone house, left to him by Geoff. He has moved back to Devon. Not sure where, but no doubt he can be found on Facebook.

Josephine, the coach escort, has returned to England. She now has two grandchildren, Sophia, and Luc, and wishes to be there to see them grow up. However, she occasionally travels to Rhodes to visit her mother who, now quite elderly, prefers the climate on the island to the English weather.

Ruth and Bertie spent the winter in Chilham. They had turned the cottage into a simple, but comfortable home, with extras, like underfloor heating and a large sunny conservatory. They enjoyed babysitting for Marcus and Claire when needed, but loved going into Canterbury to the theatre, or have lunch with friends. There would be a craft group again in the spring, Peggy was organising it all. Ruth and Bertie would book into Melenos for a week or two, join the group for dinner some evenings, and Ruth would teach silk painting.

I think that is the end.

****

AFTERWORD

Again, I would like to thank the people of Rhodes, Greek, expats, tourists, who have allowed me to use their story in my novels. It has been great fun. Thank you also to Peter O'Shea (the egg man) and Simon Goodman, my friends from Malta. And Holly Schofield for the trip to Symi, inspiring this story.

To Mary Duff, Mary Kelly and Anne Fitzroy for proofreading in Portugal and Gloria McIlveen here on Rhodes.

My thanks also to my son Desmond O'Leary here on Rhodes for initial encouragement and practical help with my writing.

To Patrick in Wigan and James in Vancouver Island for listening to Mother bleating on about it all.

As always, to my daughter Josephine Miranda for inviting me to Lindos, without which my Lindos trilogy would never have happened. Jk

****

ABOUT THE AUTHOR

Josephine Kelly was born in London. At fifteen she left home to follow her dream of working on a farm. In Bedford she met her first husband, Patrick O'Leary and married before her eighteenth birthday.

They moved to Northampton, and when the youngest of her four children started school Josephine gained a Certificate of Education, via Leicester University. She subsequently taught at St. Pauls V.C. school in Semilong, and tutored adult craft subjects with H.F. Holidays. Before retiring Josephine spent some years managing Sheltered Housing, both in the public and private sectors.

Her connection with Rhodes Island began when, in retirement, she was invited to join her daughter, Josephine Miranda, in Lindos. The rest is history.

A picture paints a thousand words.

AMBROSIA www.lindostreasures.com/ambrosia

ARCHIPELAGOS - FB@Archipelagos Restaurant Bar

DELIGHT   https://www.facebook.com/delightrestaurantlindos/

ELECRA STUDIOS LINDOS www.electra-studios.gr

GIORGOS BAR
www.exclusivelylindos.com/indexphp/pages/giogos-bar

INFINITY WEDDINGS   www.infinityweddingslindos.co.uk

_KATSIDONIS jewellery, watches, service, info@katsidonis.gr

KALYPSO BAR www.calypsolindos.gr

LIZ LOCKWOOD   www.elizabethlockwood.co.uk

LIGHT HOUSE   www.prasonisilighthouse.com

MEDEAST RESTAURANT   medeastrestaurant@yahoo.gr

MELANI TOURIST BOAT Facebook Living on Rhodes together

MELENOS HOTEL   www.melenoslindos.com

NEFELI RESTAURANT   www.lindosrestaurant.gr

PALESTRA RESTAURANT – FB@ PALESTRA-DI-LINDOS

ROMEO RESTAURANT   www.romeo.gr

SYMI DREAM   www.symidream.com

Takis Leather Shop, Symi Island

Lightning Source UK Ltd.
Milton Keynes UK
UKHW021445130422
401514UK00008B/1775